The Highest
Level *of*
Enlightenment

ALSO BY DR. DAVID R. HAWKINS, M.D., Ph.D.

Books

Book of Slides: The Complete Collection Presented at the 2002–2011 Lectures with Clarifications

Discovery of the Presence of God: Devotional Nonduality

The Ego Is Not the Real You: Wisdom to Transcend the Mind and Realize the Self

The Eye of the I: From Which Nothing Is Hidden

Healing and Recovery

I: Reality and Subjectivity

In the World, But Not of It: Transforming Everyday Experience into a Spiritual Path

Letting Go: The Pathway of Surrender

The Map of Consciousness Explained: A Proven Energy Scale to Actualize Your Ultimate Potential

Power vs. Force: The Hidden Determinants of Human Behavior

Reality, Spirituality and Modern Man

Success Is for You: Using Heart-Centered Power Principles for Lasting Abundance and Fulfillment

Transcending the Levels of Consciousness: The Stairway to Enlightenment

Truth vs. Falsehood: How to Tell the Difference

The Wisdom of Dr. David R. Hawkins: Classic Teachings on the Spiritual Truth and Enlightenment

Audio Programs

How to Surrender to God

Live Life as a Prayer

The Map of Consciousness Explained

Please visit:

Hay House USA: www.hayhouse.com®
Hay House Australia: www.hayhouse.com.au
Hay House UK: www.hayhouse.co.uk
Hay House India: www.hayhouse.co.in

* * *

The Highest Level *of* Enlightenment

TRANSCEND THE LEVELS *of* CONSCIOUSNESS FOR TOTAL SELF-REALIZATION

* * *

David R. Hawkins, M.D., Ph.D.

HAY HOUSE, INC.
Carlsbad, California • New York City
London • Sydney • New Delhi

Published in the United States by: Hay House, Inc.: www.hayhouse.com®
Published in Australia by: Hay House Australia Pty. Ltd.: www.hayhouse.com.au
Published in the United Kingdom by: Hay House UK, Ltd.: www.hayhouse.co.uk
Published in India by: Hay House Publishers India: www.hayhouse.co.in

Project editor: Sally Mason-Swaab
Cover design: Barbara LeVan Fisher
Interior design: Lisa Vega

**Cataloging-in-Publication Data is on file at
the Library of Congress**

Tradepaper ISBN: 978-1-4019-6499-3
E-book ISBN: 978-1-4019-6507-5

10 9 8 7 6 5 4 3 2 1
1st edition, February 2024

Printed in the United States of America

This product uses papers sourced from responsibly managed forests. For more information, see www.hayhouse.com.

CONTENTS

✳ ❋ ✳

INTRODUCTION

* ✳ *

Welcome to *The Highest Level of Enlightenment*. You have just embarked on a journey that is likely different than any you've ever experienced. This journey begins with the extraordinary life history of a remarkable spiritual teacher, Dr. David Hawkins. Best known for the work he has done in kinesiology and energy calibration, he has discovered a powerful tool you can use to uncover the truth or falsity of any statement, regardless of your opinions or feelings about it.

The ramifications of this system of measurement are immense. Notable spiritual leaders like Wayne Dyer have been known to fly across the globe to attend Dr. Hawkins's sold-out lectures on numerous occasions, taking copious notes throughout. From the early age of three, Dr. Hawkins found himself gifted and cursed with a life riddled with paradoxes and unanswered questions. Through his search, he experienced both heaven and hell, but ultimately, along his own tumultuous path, he found true enlightenment.

He remains here, dedicated to bringing the energy and wisdom of his enlightened path to those who are ready to listen not with their minds but with their hearts. As you follow Dr. Hawkins's teachings, it's important that you understand that reading goes well beyond the mind. In the framework of energy that Dr. Hawkins has pioneered, the act of reading and even being in the presence of higher energy consciousness has a profound effect on your energy and the journey of your soul.

You may find that at first, your mind does not fully grasp the concepts that he is sharing, but rest assured, your soul comprehends every utterance. In fact, based on Dr. Hawkins's explorations, the act of simply reading the material in and of itself can positively impact your own energy and spiritual growth experience. We encourage you to read this book repeatedly and often. As you do, you will find layers of wisdom and insights unfolding that are clearly of a higher consciousness. At times it'll feel like a jigsaw puzzle that your mind can't fully wrap itself around. Know then that the energy work is being done. Your ego mind struggles as your soul soars.

CHAPTER 1

A Remarkable
Journey *of*
Enlightenment

❋

The following section is taken from a 2003 workshop that Dr. Hawkins held in San Juan Capistrano. He begins by sharing his own personal journey of transformation, among other topics, a journey that seems to span well beyond one simple lifetime.

One instant avenue to God is through beauty, and it was through beauty that I found God as a child in a high Episcopal cathedral, where I was an acolyte to the bishop and a boy soprano. And the experiences of this lifetime, which I will just cover briefly, will explain some of my eccentricities and strange behaviors. It began really at age three out of nothingness, out of oblivion of what was believed at the time to be the void, the ultimate reality of void. I was a student of Buddhism, the pathway of negation for many lifetimes and you go out into nothing, because if you believe the ultimate reality is void, then what you get is void. If void was real, you could stay there. Void is not real, so you have to come back, and I found that at age three, coming out of void and suddenly—bam!—there was the realization of existence, not existence as this small, little body, as disgusting as it was laying in this wagon, which I was not pleased about, but, just the consciousness of existence; a stunning confrontation with existence.

It's like a refutation that the ultimate truth was void, because now, I get—it's existence. So I got existence, and then instantly came up the conundrum the fear of non-existence. I thought if I existed, it could have come about that I would not have come into existence, and suddenly the fear of nonexistence arose. So that was the polarity, the duality, the opposites, the conundrum of this lifetime. It took 50 years to solve it. Is the ultimate reality allness or nothingness? At consciousness level 850, it resolves itself. So that was the confrontation.

And when other children were worrying about playing games, I was concerned with existence versus nonexistence. While they played stickball, I was reading Plato and Aristotle and other great philosophers of history, and I have all the great books of the Western world at home. The preoccupation with the great books of the Western world is really, What is truth, and how can one get to know truth? And if you calibrate the great books, the greatest thinkers that have ever lived, all the great philosophers throughout all of time, the great books of the Western world calibrate at about 468. It's stuck in the intellect, which is the problem with trying to bridge the gap between religion and spirituality and science, because science only can go so far. We'll get to the calibrated levels of consciousness, but you'll see that science is stuck in the 400s. Einstein was 499. Freud was 499. Sir Isaac Newton, 499. That's as far as the intellect can go.

So then, after being very, very religious, I suffered from scrupulosity. I had a dread fear of sinning, and sin, the priest mentioned, was like a spot on your soul, like this invisible screen behind you, but God can see this spot. It's enough to give you paranoia. So I would go to confession. High Episcopal is very much like Catholicism. You know, we would have confession on Saturday afternoon, and I would go as late as possible and then I'd go to the earliest mass possible. You weren't supposed to sin between confession and communion. So if I got out of confession at quarter to five, I only had to make it till 7:00, the first communion on Sunday morning, and avoid sin for 12 or 14 hours. Well, you had to guard your thoughts and be very, very careful, and you know how it is when you're trying to control your thoughts. The more you try not to think of a green camel, you know how it is. I don't want anybody to think about a green camel for five minutes.

So anyway, you're avoiding sin. And I can remember on the way to church, we had a '29 Model-A Ford, and the top was put down. Just as we got near church, there was a 30-foot billboard with a Jantzen swimming suit ad, this 30-foot blonde, curvaceous, laying there. Driven mad by testosterone, as every 14-year-old boy is, a 30-foot Jantzen swimming suit ad was enough to throw you into a terror of sin. It was with trepidation that I took communion that morning. I thought lightning could strike you.

The fear of God, huh, there's the fear of God because of not knowing the truth about God. If God was an arbitrary egomaniac that would all make, you know, be sensible. But that conception of God is what was dominant in the older, established religions. The religious institution gained a great deal of power over the populous, keeping them terrorized. So God was the ultimate tool of terrorization. The ultimate wickedness, actually demonic, vicious, retaliatory, jealous, paranoid, unstable, insecure God coming out of the Old Testament. He had his favorites, and if you weren't one of his favorites, I was going to say God help you, but . . .

* * *

At 12 or 14, I had the longest paper route in the state of Wisconsin, 18 miles out in the country. This one time, it was 10-below zero, blizzard conditions, and all my papers blew away. It was pitch-black, way after time to be home, and I was a long, long way from home. The bicycle fell over on the ice; the papers blew away in the dark. And I started to cry. Frustration. And I thought, *I'll dig into this snowbank.* Well, in Wisconsin at the end of January, the snow is 10 feet high, so I dug into a hole in the snowbank. Broke through the crust and climbed in there.

All of a sudden, an incredible state overcame me. I don't want to think about it too much because it starts it up again. The infinite presence of an exquisite peace—it was like the essence of love. Any personal self just dissolved. There was only the totality of this infinite presence, not different than that which I am, truth the Self was the Self of this presence, which existed before all time began and will be there when all time has ended. Before all universes and after all universes, there'll be that. That was all non-verbal. It was only the knowingness of being at one with that presence.

Beyond all time and the condition lasted for eons. The conditions beyond time are not measurable in conceptual ideas of time, so it went on for an infinite period—infinite in worldly concepts. When it came to an end, the father— my father—was shaking my foot. He was afraid I was going to freeze to death. And I saw that he believed in death, and if I didn't come back in the body, he would think I'd died, and I saw he would go through great grief. So, because of my love for him, I did come back.

So then later on in later life, one time I was walking out in the woods by myself, and it came to me—the total knowingness of the total suffering of all of mankind in all of its totality throughout all of time. I don't know how to explain it to you. It came out of a knowingness and a stunning confrontation that was incredible. I looked at the totality of the agony of all men. Whew, God. In that moment, I became an atheist. Because the belief in God in those days was that God was the creator of everything, including toenail fungus. God was the creator of everything, so not only is he a bad guy, but he's the creator of everything, and all this horrible, horrific suffering, he created that too. Well, I could not believe in a God like that. You see, so this entity was already devoted to truth and recognized that that was not truth. Lacking sophistication, I didn't realize that what I was looking at was the creation of the human ego, but it was blamed on God, which still happens on every night's newsreel: Why did God allow this to happen to my child, to be run over by the bus? Right? He never heard of karma? From the atheist, then, there was the search for truth through psychoanalysis. I went through incredible psychoanalysis. I read all the great philosophers and great literature of the world and read about Zen and various things, but there was a progressive despair. It got worse about my mid-30s or so, and it was like an obsession to get to the core and the essence of truth, whether there was such a truth or not. I didn't call it God anymore. It's as though life had no meaning, it wasn't significant to live life unless one could reach this. Otherwise life was sort of a silly behaviorism, a conditioned reflex. You could do without it—it didn't have any real profound significance, unless you could find some core of existential truth that would give it significance. If it's only lived for the sake of moment to moment, then it's just an animal life and what's the point of going through the suffering of it. You might as well quit now.

There was this drive to reach the core and reach the bottom, and in my mid-30s this became an obsession. And driving and driving and driving for it, I got to an inner core of despair and black despair, and then the opposite of what I'd experienced in the snowbank. I got to experience the lower levels of hell. The higher levels of hell were dreadful. And what most people think of as hell are the higher levels. Jacks for openers, that isn't even hell, people's tongues being torn out and tormented, I mean that's nothing at all. Then it starts to get bad, and the pits of hell, like the heights of heaven, are formless. So you go past the form and the dread and the terror, and there's a knowingness that Dante saw. Dante—how he knew it I don't know. There's a knowingness beyond this point, give up all hope forevermore, and then you go to the real depths, which are timeless eons of agony beyond, agony of the spirit. And at the depths of the agony of the spirit, there's no hope of ever coming out of it. There's no means of doing so.

At the depths of it all, this ardent, dedicated atheist said, "If there is a God, I ask him for help." And then oblivion, and then an awakening, I don't know how much later—a day or two, six hours, I have no idea—in which everything had been transformed to the opposite. There was no person left. There's no person talking now. People say, "What are you going to talk about?" How would I know till I hear it? There isn't any, like, central control unit making a decision of where we're going to go and what we're going to say. It all happens as a consequence of the totality of the field.

So the reality of the presence within is absolute silence. Everything moves and talks and does what it does spontaneously. As you can see, the body moves about on its own. It has nothing to do with any person at all. People talk to it because that's the way it is in the world. It moves spontaneously. Everything happens of its own. Everything is being said of its own. Everything comes out of an absolute silent awareness and knowingness of what it is. Everything becomes the expression of its own potentiality. And that's what's speaking to you today.

Classically, the gnosis of the Purusha, of the teacher, is the presence within, which spontaneously expresses through the physicality. Everyone is interested in spiritual advancement, and so I try to speak of the things that I think would speed up everybody's intention. The biggest block, as you will see when we get to the levels of consciousness, has to do with the idea of causality. You'll see that consciousness in our civilization is characteristically in the 400s, which is the intellect, and the intellect is based on the whole idea of causality. There is a *this* causing a *that*. So if we get beyond the illusion of causality, we can jump into the 500s, where you see that everything is happening as a consequence of the totality. Nothing is causing anything. So then we have to explain if nothing is causing anything, then how does anything come to be what it is?

So instead I'll tell you the highest truth that's knowable. Everything that's happening of its own spontaneously as a consequence of the infinite power of the field, you see. There is the content of the field, and then there is the field. The power is that of the field. The presence of God is like an enormous electromagnetic field of such enormous power that it keeps together the entire universe, every atom, every molecule. Its immensity and its power is beyond imagination.

This field, then, dominates all of creation. Everything is then subject to the power of the field. So the spirit, as it evolves over the lifetimes, over the eons, really, acquires, you might say, through spiritual intention and decision like a magnetic charge of greater or lesser intensity of this or that polarity of this negativity and that positivity, every decision, so it's like the spiritual will by its overall intention, it's spiritual intention that dominates and designs one's karmic inheritance. It's by spiritual intention, then, that we set our own karmic inheritance. People say, "I don't believe in karma." Well, I'll tell you, what you are is your karma. What you're looking at is your karma.

As Dr. Hawkins shared his remarkable life story with you, he touched on concepts like duality, the field, and karma. Some of these concepts may be new to you or may carry different meanings in relation to Dr. Hawkins's teachings. He will further discuss each of these concepts in much greater detail in the upcoming chapters.

In the next chapter, he will provide you with a detailed explanation of a powerful spiritual tool, The Map of Consciousness®, telling you how he created it and how it may be used to best serve you on your spiritual path.

CHAPTER 2

An Introduction to the Map *of* Consciousness®

Through a technique known as muscle testing, or kinesiology, Dr. Hawkins has done extensive research on the path of the human spirit and has subsequently created a map of consciousness. This map calibrates levels that correlate to specific processes of consciousness, emotions, perceptions, attitudes, world views, and spiritual beliefs. Each is given a numeric value that reflects the condition's inherent energy.

The scale begins at the low energy level of 20 and reaches to the highest human energy calibration level of 1,000. The critical response point on the scale of consciousness calibrates at level 200, which is a level associated with integrity and courage. Therefore, any states below 200, states such as shame, grief, apathy, guilt, fear, desire, anger, and pride are energy drainers and require force in order to exist. On the other hand, those states on the scale above 200, states being courage, neutrality, willingness, acceptance, reason, love, joy, peace, and enlightenment, are power-based states that are life-sustaining and spiritually supportive.

Before we proceed any further, it's best that you understand how this map was created and the methodology that was used to substantiate Dr. Hawkins's findings. Muscle testing, or kinesiology, is now considered a well-established science and is based upon the testing of an all-or-none muscle response stimulus. Originally researched by Dr. George Goodheart in the early '70s and later given wider application by Dr. John Diamond, this process is a clear demonstration that muscles instantly become weak when the body is exposed to harmful stimuli. Two people are required to begin this testing procedure. One acts as a test subject by holding out his or her arm laterally, parallel to the ground. The second person presses down with two fingers on the wrist of the extended arm and says, "Resist." The subject then resists the downward pressure with all of his or her strength. This is the basic procedure.

A statement may be made by either party. Then while the subject holds that statement in mind, his or her arm strength is tested by the tester's downward pressure, again applied by two fingers on the wrist of the subject. If the statement is negative, false, or reflects a calibration below 200, the test subject will go weak. If the statement is positive, however, or the answer is yes, calibrating over 200, the subject will go strong. It should be noted that the questions asked must be put in the form of a declarative statement in order to verify truth or falsity. For example, if you are 35 years old, you might say, "I am 35 years old" and have someone press down on your extended arm. You will stay strong. If you then say, "I am 38 years old" and have someone press down on your arm, you'll instantly go weak. Also, it should be noted that the parties involved must be impersonal in the procedure. Avoid distractions. Remove eyeglasses, hats, jewelry, and watches, especially quartz, and have a desire to attain the truth on the matter at hand.

This procedure sounds all too simple. However, the truth is its spirit is simple. It's the human ego that certainly likes to complicate things. Dr. Hawkins has researched kinesiology and substantiated his findings for over 29 years. As he will articulate, this method of calibration is very powerful and can prove useful in making discernments in any area of your life. All that is required of you is simply integrity and the desire to know and experience the truth.

So here's man struggling through the ages. Just think of over the centuries how many ships went down and how many sailors died at the bottom of the sea for lack of a compass. Well, that's just the paradigm of what mankind has gone through, with no capacity to tell truth from falsehood, then man stumbles and cannot tell the sheep from the wolf. So, as Christ said, look out for the wolf in sheep's clothing, but he didn't teach kinesiology and tell you how to discern which sheep's clothing has a wolf in it.

For the first time we discovered how to tell truth from falsehood. That was so shocking that I really didn't know what to do with it for quite a while. And then we began to verify it with thousands of experiments, and we tried it with large classes. We tried it with research groups. We ended up calibrating the levels of consciousness, which is well known now as the Map of Consciousness®. We discovered that things that make you go weak on a scale of consciousness could be calibrated numerically, and so we ended up with a logarithmic scale of consciousness that goes from 1 to 1,000, against which we can calibrate the level of truth of anything.

As I said, I didn't say anything about all this for, you know, 30 years. The problem was how to present it in such a way that is comprehensible and how will it correlate with traditional spiritual trainings and teachings and belief systems. So kinesiology then led to a way in which you could create a ladder to go from the intellect to the ordinary mind to a spiritual reality. And of course, the person who gets caught in the intellect can't get beyond it. In fact, only maybe 4 percent of the human population ever gets beyond intellect, gets beyond the calibrated level of the 400s. So the intellect, on the one hand, is the great savior of mankind. It certainly was for Western civilization. But it then becomes the very block to spiritual awareness.

We then discovered that with kinesiology one could actually calibrate levels of consciousness and created this scale that goes from 1 to 1,000, and we could ask the energy of something is over a certain number. So what came out of it was an arbitrary scale. It turned out to be 1 to 1,000, and the numbers turn out to be logarithmic because they become so huge that we had to go back to the log of the number. And we discovered things that made your arm go strong on a scale, anybody can do this at home. You see on a scale of one to five, you know, this is a two or a three or a four. Anybody can construct their own scale, but with a lot of research, we devised a scale that's pretty useful, much like a centigrade scale of temperature. We found that anything that makes your arm go strong with kinesiology calibrated over 200. Everything that made your arm go weak calibrated under 200. So then we'd say, on a scale of truth, you know, does this calibrate over 100, 200, 300, and suddenly your arm would go strong.

By experimentation with large groups of people over a considerable amount of time, we verified a very reliable scale of consciousness 1 to 1,000, and anything that calibrates over 200 is true or integrous or supports life. And that which is not integrous, that which is false, makes your arm go weak and calibrated under 200. Well, that was certainly extremely useful. So we could hold up something in front of an audience, and we could divide the audience, and we did it many times. You know, I've had an audience of 1,000 people, we divided it up into 500 couples.

One is the test subject and the other plays the part of the doctor, you know, and then we hold various things over their solar plexus or we can hold something up and have the audience look at it. One time we did it in Korea, for instance, and we were just teaching kinesiology, and we had a large class, and I didn't know what they were going to hold up. We divided it up into ones and twos, and Dr. Moon held up a bag of some kind of green veggie, and we all looked at it and everybody went strong. Then she held up an identical-looking bag of the same green veggie, and everybody looked at it and went weak.

Then I said, "So what was in it?" She said, "Well, the first one was organic cabbage and the second one was raised with pesticides." So no physical contact, you see, just the contact through consciousness itself to really hold in mind something, you can then test it with kinesiology. You can say this is above 200 or this is below 200. You can say bin Laden is over 200 or he's under 200. You can say Saddam Hussein is over 200 or under 200. In other words, you can end up calibrating anything that exists anywhere in time or place, really by holding it in mind. This seems sort of magical to people who are not familiar with consciousness, but when you realize that consciousness is what dominates all of experience, dominates all of life, dominates all of decisions, dominates everything in life as we experience it, it shouldn't be surprising. People who live within the Newtonian paradigm of form may find this quite surprising because they are looking at causality and looking at a very limited world, but they're looking at the world of form and the world of forests and existence, and life comes out of power.

So the infinite reality out of which life arises, then, is an infinite power that classically has been called God, despite people's not wanting to have the term used because it makes them uncomfortable. It makes me uncomfortable that people are made uncomfortable by the term, but divinity, that sounds less objectionable. Anyway, there is an infinite field of consciousness, which has also been described by advanced physics, you understand. David Bohm, to my mind, has the best understanding of physics because experientially he described that which is literally the experience out of the unmanifest arises the manifest, and you see a recapitulation of the story of creation, and as one goes into that awareness oneself, one sees all that exists is arising out of an infinite power out of which the capacity to exist arises.

One either assumes that one arose out of spontaneous combustion somewhere within linear time, or one begins to realize that creation and evolution are one and the same thing. There's an appreciation that that which exists must arise out of an infinite power. See, that which we accept as a given without looking at it. You say, "How does anything come into existence? How does even the capacity to be aware or conscious come into existence?" One can strain the intellect and try to look at an infinite progression of causality, which of course is the classic way of doing it, to go back through causes to a primary cause, but then one ends up at the limitation of the ego because beyond primary cause what is the primary cause. And you discover that in an infinite sequence of causes the primary is of a different class. You have to jump the class.

So the source of existence, then, is the presence of divinity, of the present moment, that existence is continuous because the presence of divinity is continuous. One's existence is constantly being sustained by the infinite power of the field out of which existence becomes a possibility. The value of the calibrated levels of consciousness was we could integrate that with spiritual history, with common human experience, with psychology, psychiatry, and we found that human emotions could be calibrated. And so we calibrated what is the level of fear—what's the level of depression, apathy, hopelessness, anger, pride—which in psychoanalysis were called the emergency emotions: fear, anxiety, or hate. We found that they all calibrated below 200, and so we were able to calibrate the negative emotions.

Then we find that which psychoanalysis calls the welfare emotions—integrity, caringness, love, ambition, dedication, helpfulness—were calibrated, and then we get to the intellect, the capacity to comprehend the nature of things within the Newtonian paradigm of reality. And that's the world of the intellect.

✳ ✳ ✳

America right now, for instance, calibrates the highest of any country in the world. The consciousness level of America as a nation is 421, which is above and beyond any other country on the planet at the moment. So if we look at the nature of what is a civilization that calibrates at 421, we see learning, school, intellect, college, reading, reason, logic, computers, and the world of science. So we see that our life is ruled by what we at least presume to be reason and logic and proof and scientific evidence. And so our society stresses education probably above all else. Education is the road that will decide your career, your income, and your social status, and influence your whole social life, etc., where you live, it's probably all going to come out of your education to some degree.

So we see the 400s are quite powerful. The 400s have given us science, and modern man owes its survival considerably to science. You know, when I started in medicine, most of the diseases that we treated and were quite concerned about don't even exist anymore—diphtheria and typhoid and polio—and when I was in charge of an infectious disease hospital, all the diseases that people died of—malaria, encephalitis, meningitis, and all of the things we treated—don't even exist anymore. So science has been the great benefactor of society. Now, with antibiotics, nobody dies of any of those things anymore, and we've got antidotes for them and many of those diseases have absolutely disappeared.

The 400s of the world is the world of the college, the professor, the university. It's the world as we know it. What happens when we get to the 500s is that we enter a new dimension. We go from the Newtonian levels of reason, and we begin to enter a nonmeasurable domain of the 500s. Five hundred is the level of love. Four hundreds has to do with logic and reason, and it talks about love and will tell you that love is good for you and all this kind of stuff, but that is not what love is. That's talking about love.

✳ ✳ ✳

Now, at level 500, which is reached by 4 percent of the population, is the capacity for actual love. At 500, love takes on a different experiential reality. It's not the emotion of love. When people talk about love, they're talking about an emotion, that which goes from this to that, I love you, you love me, and therefore it can be lost. That person could stop loving you, and if that person is the source of your happiness, now you're going to be quite desperate. And of course, love relationships that go downhill often result in suicide and homicide. In other words, it can cause quite a violent reaction. And one is always vulnerable, so to be in love in that sense, then you're putting your happiness outside of yourself.

As you get to the 500s, the source of happiness is not outside yourself but comes from within. So love at calibrated level 500 now changes into a way of being in the world. Spiritual love is a way of being. It's the way you are within the world, what you are to the world. It's now beyond emotion. It doesn't depend on emotion, and it's independent of the world. If the other person loves you, so much the better, and if they don't, you continue to love them anyway. So I love my kitty no matter what, and if my kitty suddenly stops loving me, that's the kitty's loss because I still love the kitty, you know, and he'll get out of his bad mood. So we become that which sort of nurtures life. The energy field of somebody in the 500s now begins to radiate out and support life.

Interestingly, all the people in the 400s that think they're surviving of their own impetus, by their own output, by their own logic, etc., are only doing so because, like a quark, they are afloat in a field that is held by the benevolence of the 500s and up. It's the presence of divinity that allows the child to play with his intellect. I mean, I'm looking at the adult with the child with the intellect. Now, it's the power of the field now that sustains the person. So in the 500s, then, we see a transformation that cannot be explained in Newtonian terms. So the scientific reductionist is stuck because you can't really explain love or any of the things that are not measurable. Radical reductionist science says if it can't be measured or weighed, you know, it's not real. Of course, that's a rather naïve absurdity, but the scientist who says that lives completely and totally within his own subjective experiential self, so even while he's sitting there saying that in some kind of an absurd tone of voice, it's because he's convinced subjectively that's the truth. So, it's a subjective statement.

So then, one comes into the awareness that all reality and experience of reality is radically subjective. So that subjectivity in the 500s, then, demarcates love and from a 500 to 540, the capacity to love increases very powerfully. At 540 it changes now to unconditional love. So 500 is loving, but it also still has some conditionality to it. At 540 love becomes unconditional. Well, what's the practical importance of that? The practical importance of that is, let's say alcoholism was hopeless throughout all of man's history, and nobody ever recovered from it except a few people in history who had fallen into some religious beliefs, and it was when Bill Wilson went into a transformative spiritual experience himself and discovered the basic spiritual reality out of which the 12-step programs have arisen. We discovered that AA, for instance, calibrates at 540. So the great 12-step movement that has transformed a good part of America and worked silently in the background even though people are not aware of it, the 12 Steps, which have become useful in treating all kinds ·of human problems, from weight problems, to suicide, to depression, to alcohol, drugs, and violence, and many other human problems, require an energy field at 540 to cure them.

You can't cure them in the 400s. Science can't cure addictions, and love itself can't cure them, because your mother can love you, your wife can love you, your kids can love you, and you still drink yourself to death. So 500 or 520 or 530 won't do it. No. It takes a power. So it's the power of the field, then, that sustains. So we can scientifically validate, then, that an energy field of 540 can bring about the recovery of millions of people from a hopeless and incurable disease. First time it happened, it was with psychoanalyst Carl Jung, though it would also happen occasionally to people throughout history. When Rowland Hazard III went to see Carl Jung because of his problem with alcohol, he recovered for a while and then relapsed. He went back to Switzerland and saw Carl Jung again, who calibrated at 520, had spiritual awareness. It was also his humility that accounted for the birth of the later phenomena; he told Rowland, "Alas, I cannot help you; neither my science nor my art can help you." He told Rowland that, in history, some people have gone to spiritual programs, and it had been recorded that occasionally here and there throughout history people had recovered.

So Rowland went back in a profound state of depression and hopelessness and threw himself into the Oxford Groups, which were pretty much the precursor of AA. And it started the whole awareness in our society that powerful spiritual programs and powerful spiritual truth can actually cure physical illness. It's the field that cures it, and subscribing to the field and spiritual truth. So humanity, society, discovered experientially, and for all to see that which was hopeless, the miraculous was possible by virtue only of spiritual power. And so intuitively people began to get that that is power, which is different than force. With force, you say, "If you don't stop drinking, we'll put you in jail," and I've treated, you know, 10,000 alcoholic people and etc. over my lifetime. You can put them in jail over and over again, take their car away, take their driver's license away, their wife leaves them, their family leaves them, they get fired from their job, and all of that—which is all the exercise of force—has absolutely no effect whatsoever, no effect whatsoever.

And then the person will go into a field at 540. Everybody says, "Hey, wow, man, glad you're here," give him a hug, and suddenly the guy feels a shot of something different, and from that moment on, many a person has recovered. So that's a vivid clinical demonstration of the energy field that we describe at 540. Other things have appeared since then, of sort of a widespread experience, because I'm looking for verification through human experience. *A Course in Miracles* appeared out of nowhere, and *A Course in Miracles* calibrates at 600. So then began the demonstration that even greater phenomena that people could recover not only from addictions but also from other grave illnesses by virtue of following spiritual pathways. And *A Course in Miracles* grew pretty much like AA. Groups formed spontaneously. There's nobody in charge. It doesn't own any buildings. So the spread of spiritual truth, then, has given a large percent of the population in the country demonstration of the experience of what spiritual truth is and what it can do and what it looks like when a person lives it, that it can cure incurable illnesses, and in *A Course in Miracles* we've seen people, of course, who have recovered from every illness known to mankind.

However, it doesn't mean you're going to negate whatever karma you may have to face in this lifetime. You may transcend it or you may not. So we can translate karma into whatever the person would like to experience it as. The mechanistic person will say, "Where's your genes and your chromosomes?" and you say, okay, that's fine, and actually the genes and the chromosomes are the effect of your karma. They're not the cause of it. You know, they're the consequence. So when you get beyond causality, you see that everything is manifesting and becoming that which it is as a result of the field. So as a result of the field, you've automatically chosen these particular genes and chromosomes to express whatever tendency or propensity you've come into this lifetime with. That sounds somewhat theoretical to the average Westerner.

To the average Easterner, you know, karma is a given, and everybody lives their life according to it, and it's one of the profound truths of everyday life. And notice, the world seems to be somewhat oblivious to it. You know, as a practical spiritual teacher I'll say, avoid everything that makes you go weak with kinesiology and pursue that which makes you go strong, because that which makes you go weak with kinesiology has done so throughout the ages, through many thousands of years. The Vidyas arose maybe 10,000 years ago, and what we consider to be modern spiritual belief systems or religious belief systems, were ancient 10,000 years ago, because the experience of the presence of God, which we call the experience of the mystic, has been a recurrence throughout all of history, but, are relatively rare. The chances are maybe 1 in 10 million statistically, if we study kinesiology.

But spontaneously it suddenly occurs, and it's been the same throughout all of history. And spiritual reality never changes. Although religions may differ in their belief systems, they're only differing in their belief systems. Any of the bases upon which they differ cannot be proven, because every religion arises out of the subjectivity of that which is really descriptively the mystic. The self-realized reports the same phenomena over and over. There's only one truth, and therefore, as it is expressed from consciousness itself, it is always the same. So the great avatars, the great enlightened sages of time, always say the same thing, because there is only one reality, and there is none other, and it's not possible to stay with truth and describe it other than what it is. So the origins of all the great religions are the same, and so then we went on to study various religions and you can calibrate the levels of movies, books, writers, TV programs. Everything then represents a greater or a lesser degree of spiritual energy, and the greater the spiritual orientation, the alignment with truth, the higher the calibration.

And so we have this calibrated scale of consciousness, which its greatest usefulness is merely to say yes or not yes. So you would say, "This spiritual teacher is integrous and useful for my life," and you get a yes or a not yes. Or you might say, "It's too soon; maybe I should wait with this one," it'll say yes or not yes. So one can use it for guidance, and spiritual students who are really committed to transcending the ego on reaching the higher spiritual states have found it quite useful.

We've found that the reason we used 1,000 as the top of the scale is we asked what is the highest consciousness that has ever existed on the planet. We got 1,000 is the limit of possibility within the human domain, that the human nervous system cannot really handle the energy that calibrates much over 1,000, that the Buddha, Christ, Krishna, and all the great avatars calibrated at 1,000. It's not really possible to survive with a—you might say the voltage is too high for the human nervous system when you get over 1,000, and even getting to 1,000 can be quite agonizing. What we call enlightenment occurred at a level that calibrated at 600. When a person goes into 600, they go into the levels of love—first conditional love, then unconditional love, then many become interested in spiritual pathways and meditation and spiritual techniques, and they begin to pursue them with greater and greater dedication. And as they do, they begin to experience life in a transformative, completely different context.

In the high 500s, which are quite amazing, one is over-come by the sheer beauty of everything. The only reality that exists is love. There is only love, and all you see is love, and all you experience is love and beauty and harmony, and the miraculous begins to happen spontaneously and eventually becomes continuous. A lot of people who've done *A Course in Miracles* go into that transformative state. You drive into the city and you think of a parking space, and as you get there, there's a parking space right in front of Lincoln Center—the one and only parking space—just as you pull up, a car pulls out and you pull in. When this first begins to happen, you sort of remark about it. After a while, you begin to experience that that's the way life is. It's the continuous miraculous. The miraculous is ongo-ing and continuous. And everybody becomes stunningly beautiful and handsome, stunningly attractive. One's in love—no, not falls in love. One is in love with everything and everyone all the time. And one can only see the beauty and the perfection of everything.

And then the state may reach in the very high 500s, ecstasy. One can start going into states of indescribable ecstasy, like the opening of a brilliance within one's con-sciousness, and the ecstasy is continuous. At that point you can't function in the world anymore. The ecstasy then, Ramakrishna described it—I remember going through it myself—forget functioning in the world. You can dance. You can dance in like an expression of exquisite ecstasy at the joy of one's existence, and one cannot function. And then one has to surrender that to God, so each step along the way of the levels of consciousness is surrender-ing whatever is presenting itself to God. Finally, even the state of ecstasy, one has to surrender the state of ecstasy to God, and then one hits level 600, which is a state of infinite silence, bliss, and a profound peace beyond all understanding. The peace of God is beyond psychological peace or emotional peace. It's a different dimension. And in that state, you don't have to eat, breathe, function. One blisses out outside of time. Sat Chit Ananda it's called classically. And if things are favorable, the body will eventually get fed, move up, and walk around and survive. If the conditions are not favorable to that circumstance, which, frankly, is irrelevant, then it just topples over eventually. So about 50 percent of the people who go into a latent state, frankly, leave.

The one awareness that is quite obvious in that state is that you have permission to leave. You can leave right now, in fact. One has permission. What's going to keep the body going? Well, you see, there's no needs and no wants. Everything is complete and total. The bliss of the state is that everything is complete. So from that moment on, if the body survives, you don't ever really need anything anymore. People say what do you want. Well, I don't want anything. What do you need? Well, I don't need anything. Certain things would be nice, but you don't need them. And so one is then independent of the world. What the world says or does is really quite irrelevant. At that point it's impossible to function, I remember in that state, so what happens if you survive is most people leave the world, which is, yes, what I did. So you pack up everything and throw all your tools in the back of your old truck, and you say good-bye and you leave, which is what I did. So I left the biggest practice in the country and a very elite lifestyle, etc., and drove to a small town. You know, in the refrigerator there'd be a banana, two Pepsis, and a piece of cheese, and that was fine. I mean, what more do you need? People come in and say, "You don't have any food in here."

You think, What are they talking about there's no food in here? Because you don't need anything. So you get a cot in the dime store and you get a box to put a candle on, and you've got an apple and a piece of cheese and you're all set.

In this chapter, Dr. Hawkins provided you with a greater understanding of the Map of Consciousness® and the calibration process. He painted a fascinating and vivid picture of the emotional and spiritual climate that exists at every step of the energy evolution process. As you proceed on your daily activities, you may wish to begin witnessing the various choices that you and the world around you make on a constant, often unconscious basis. What might the calibration level be on the Map of Consciousness®? Subsequently, you may wish to begin experimenting with kinesiological testing.

As you gain a greater understanding of this powerful process, you can begin to use it as part of your regular routine. When flipping through a potential new book, for instance, you may wish to test whether it would be a beneficial addition to your current library. You may wish to test the shows that you watch on television or a myriad of other areas that you would like to further explore. As you practice this technique, you will gain a greater sense of the power conductors that feed you in your life and learn to leave any power drainers behind.

CHAPTER 3

Following the
Path *of* Devotional
Nonduality

* ✳ *

*When we choose to experience life differently, the entire
planet will open up before our perceptual eyes. Thus the change
starts and ends not in the externals that too strongly govern
our current existence, but in our perceptions. In this chapter,
Dr. Hawkins will cover a full array of topics. He will begin by
giving us an opportunity to take a leap of faith and reperceive
our sense of God or the divine. He explains that God is not a
wrathful or vengeful persona who is the cause of our shame,
fears, and suffering. In truth, he explains that divinity is an
impersonal electromagnetic field that resonates love and is the
infinite source of all creation.*

*He clarifies that we need to move beyond our sequential,
linear perceptions as we find ourselves trapped in ineffective
and inaccurate misunderstandings that drive us further into
limited thinking. He illuminates the difference between power
and force, and clarifies how we have gotten caught in a weak-
ening belief system based on the polarity of opposites, black or
white, right or wrong, or, as he aptly puts it, in loving vanilla,
you don't have to hate chocolate.*

So we have a very advanced consciousness sitting in the
audience, people destined for celestial realms, heavenly

realms and enlightenment. Otherwise they wouldn't be here. You'd be at the ball game. Why would you be here?

It's because you've already chosen your destiny, and that's what makes this fascinating. I want to save you a few eons.

What is happening is this giant electromagnetic field, then, picture God as a giant electromagnetic field whose power is infinite, without parts, without neurosis, without psychosis. Not the God of the Old Testament at all. But the infinite source of all creation out of the unmanifest arises the manifest, which arises as creation, which is continuous, so that what you're witnessing is the unfolding of creation as you become aware of it, to sequential perception. But nothing is happening sequentially; only in your perception. If you walk around something and see it like this and like that and like the hologram, you're not causing it to be that at all. As you witness it sequentially, the sequencing is in your witnessing. The sequence is not in the hologram. The hologram is standing there. But as you move, you see it as though it's moving. You understand? It's like a kid's flip chart, you know, they're [the illustrations] all stationary, but as you flip through it, it looks like the guy's throwing a ball.

So you see that creation and evolution are one and the same thing. There's no conflict. No conflict is possible. Evolution is the way in which creation unfolds itself. There's this enormous field of power that contains all within it. That which has the potential to come into existence, then, is energized into existence, and its source is the infinite presence of God as creator. All things come into manifestation, and they come into the form. The form is then dependent on the intrinsic potentiality, which arises out of their karmic inheritance. The seed lies in the ground. It has the potential to become a marigold, but it's not a marigold. It's only a seed in the ground. Can anything cause it to be a marigold? Try causing it to do anything. You can't cause it to do anything. I demand that you become a marigold.

You cannot cause it because cause is force. Causation is force. Creation is power. On the other hand, a little bit of sunshine, a few drops of rain, and now you've provided the conditions in which its karmic potentiality comes into manifestation, and it only can do so because of the infinite power of the field that allows the potentiality to become an actuality. Therefore, creation is continuous. Your own karmic potentiality is what is unfolding at this moment. Everything comes into existence. Nothing has within itself the power to create its own existence. That's the ultimate stopper to the atheist, who can only now go back to causality and say, "Well, what about billiard balls?" What about them billiard balls? A hits B hits C hits D hits E, you know, right, so.

So causality, then, is an illusion. It's the core of the ego. It's the core of science. It's the core of law. And it calibrates about 460. The information to calibrate the level of causality, causality is about 460. You're going to explain this entire universe, including God, all from a consciousness level of 460? Geez, that wouldn't even get you to graduate school hardly.

Four-sixty. What about Darwin? Darwin's theory of evolution calibrates at 455. The explanation of causality is the explanation for all that exists calibrates about 460. Everything comes into existence, then, by virtue of its infinite potentiality, and the reason it manifests—it goes from potentiality into actuality—is because of the power of the field. *Power vs. Force* came out of—I'd already had an extremely enlightened experience at age 30-something or other, which took me out of the world, frankly, for many years. And I was trying to get back in the world, learning how to function again, and I saw a demonstration of kinesiology. When I saw kinesiology, I saw something different than what the other people in the room saw, which, by that time was a rather common occurrence, but . . .

When they demonstrated kinesiology, they presumed it was a local response, and it was so clear and apparent to me that it was a nonlocal response. I just thought I would denote the universe. Here's the universe, an infinite electromagnetic field, see.

* * *

The infinite reality is formless. The pathway I teach is what I call devotional nonduality. The devotion means one's love takes the form of the love for the discernment of the truth above all else. And you're driven, because it takes a very hard drive to take you out of duality into nonduality, and without the energy of devotion, inspiration, the willingness to give your all for it, including physical death. It takes death, so it takes death. And so we have an infinite field of infinite power, and within it—this is the world of formless—the invisible energy of formless. So the difference between force and power is force is linear. Force is demarcated. You see, it has a form, like a molecule or something. See, it may have ears on it, eyes, feet—anything. It has structure. It has form. Therefore, it's limited. That which has form is obviously limited. It's limited by form. That which is formless is unlimited.

Now we'll have the key to it. We'll have the $E=mc^2$ to it. This is force limited to form. This is power, which is nondual, which is infinite. Power has no limitation. In fact, the greater the demand you put on it, the greater it swells and it meets the need. Force, on the other hand, is exhausted. Force goes from here to there. It extends its own energy. You have to constantly stoke force with more and more energy. Money, bodies of soldiers, bodies of believers, their gold, their lives, their sweat, you have to pull it out, because it takes—finally the Roman Empire, which is the greatest empire the world's ever seen, after 1,000 years petered out. Ran out of gold. Bodies of women—I mean, it just ran out, and it petered out and dissolved into the countryside, and the soldiers all married the local women and said the heck with it.

So force is limited. Power, on the other hand, is unlimited. When you define what is truth, it's impossible to define truth without defining the context, and that is the reason the great books of the Western world and all the greatest philosophers that have ever lived have never solved the problems of epistemology because they never got that subtlety, yet you move from the objective to the subjective. The objective will take you up to 499, and from there you move into the subjective. The presence of God is not something one can experience through thought but experientially. It is subjective.

The levels of human consciousness are pretty much what they have been described throughout the ages, from hatred all the way up to love and then the levels of enlightenment. It's roughly comparable to the chakra system also, in that hatred is the spleen; down at the bottom we have people coming out of hatred, kill all Americans, doing all that kind of thing, so hatred comes out at, like, 70. There are lots of human beings walking around in the world and running countries that calibrate at 70. In fact, that's about the same as the Komodo dragon.

The energy of the Komodo dragon (we have permission to calibrate), he's over 40, 45, 55, 60. Sixty. The level of several of the world's recent dictators I'm holding in mind is over 45. More vicious than a Komodo dragon in human form. Christ said, "How do you tell the wolf in sheep's clothing?" Forget about wolves. They are pansies out there. I can handle a wolf anytime. But, a Komodo dragon, you're getting a little serious. Some of the world's recent dictators . . . now you're getting really serious. More vicious than a Komodo dragon, and the people vote for them. They follow them. They follow them to their death. Entities that calibrate less than a Komodo dragon. A Komodo dragon kills out of innocence. It knows that if it slathers and bites you, its bite is so venomous, he just sits back and waits a couple days and you die of bacterial infection and then he eats you. That's not really a vicious intent. He just wants to eat you. He's hungry. Can't blame a Komodo dragon for being hungry, right?

How do you tell, then, the wolf in sheep's clothing? We were warned, and we were told by their fruits we shall know them, but by the time you had a chance to check out their fruits and have a congressional investigation and have investigators go there, a great deal of time has passed and a thousand more citizens have died and they've been executed. How can you find out the truth, then, right off the bat? What we just did this morning. When I saw the kinesiologic test, I saw what you're seeing is a reaction of the field, an impersonal field. And what it is, is that consciousness itself recognizes the presence of truth. At first I thought it was truth versus falsehood. I thought it knows the truth from the false. No, it doesn't know the true from the false. It only knows the true from the not true. Oh, that's quite a difference. It knows what's true and fails to recognize what is not true. Hm. You see how that gets us out of polarity.

You see how there's a subtlety to this. It gets you out of the spiritual guilt of the polarity of the opposites, where you like this and hate that, and you feel guilty because you're supposed to be spiritual. See, there's chocolate and vanilla. You can like chocolate without hating vanilla. Got it? You don't have to hate vanilla. You just choose chocolate. You can be right wing and not hate the liberals because they're all vanilla. You can be a vanilla liberal, you don't have to hate all the conservatives because they're chocolates. You just like vanilla. I don't know how you digest that chocolate, but that's your problem, you know.

Chocolate guy says, "Vanilla is for wimpies." I mean, I don't know if you like vanilla, you like vanilla, but us guys, we like chocolate. So you can champion your cause. You can say we're the greatest and tattoo yourself, make parades, but you don't have to get into hate. You don't have to get into hate. At one level of consciousness, you have to dissolve the so-called polarity of the opposites.

As we end this chapter, Dr. Hawkins speaks of dissolving the so-called polarity of opposites. To make that first step into disempowering those that you have witnessed and your perceptions, you may wish to reflect on your life. What do you perceive as polar opposites? How often do you find yourself making such perhaps unconscious choices? Take note when you find yourself doing this. As soon as you catch yourself in this belief system, take a moment to ask yourself, Is there another way that I can perceive this? Taking time to reevaluate your choices may be one of the first steps that you take toward freeing yourself from the binding thought patterns that have kept you from your imminent spiritual progress.

CHAPTER 4

Transcending
the Ego

* ✳ *

In this chapter, Dr. Hawkins further describes the ego in relation to his teaching, his understanding of it from an enlightened perspective. He continues his discussion about the surge of integrity as a driving force in human consciousness, as Earth evolves beyond the lower-energy frequencies to the calibration level of 207. He discusses the ego and our misperceptions of it in greater detail, and he asserts that demonizing the ego is not a power-based way to work with it. The secret, he says, lies in becoming friendly with it. Doing so will be yet another powerful step in the evolution of your personal consciousness and the consciousness of humankind as a whole. Understanding the ego from the perspective of the natural evolution of our species puts it in better context. We can then reperceive it as our animal instincts that have followed us as we evolve from the reptilian state into Homo sapiens.

When we learn to perceive it from this state, judgment is not perpetuated, and a battle with the ego ceases. As you listen to the upcoming session, take note of the skepticisms or judgments that might arise. What are your current perceptions? Are they in line with truth? Or might they be the makings of your ego's wall of resistance?

The purpose of our discussion, of course, is to potentiate the evolution of consciousness, and the only purpose of the books and the lectures that I've given is to support the progression of that consciousness within the individual who's elected to pursue a higher level of consciousness. People think they're in the ordinary world of causality. They think that what they are is the product of their past. No. The reality is that it's the potentiality of what you have chosen to become that is pulling you into the present. It's not because of what you've been in the past that's pushing you up to this point. On the contrary. It's because you've elected to be that which is beyond this point that is pulling you through this point. It's because you have chosen already by spiritual intention.

So people say, "What's karma about?" Well, karma is just the automatic energy consequence of spiritual intention and spiritual decision. Well, every decision you make then affects your calibrated level of consciousness, which is a shorthand way of saying your karma. It starts first as curiosity perhaps, or hearsay. Then they find themselves automatically drawn into spiritual growth and spiritual concepts and the desire to understand them and to benefit from them. And they begin to realize that as they grow, they're benefiting the world. That which you're doing is affecting everyone. The whole world benefits from it. We can prove that also with quantum mechanics, you know, the Heisenberg principle, the collapse of the wave function then begins to affect the whole field of consciousness. Every individual who commits themselves to spiritual work is benefiting all of mankind. This is an automatic consequence of his choices and decisions, because he's collapsing the potential into the actual, which is affecting the collective consciousness of all mankind.

We found it quite interesting that when we were calibrating levels of consciousness, we asked, "What is the level of consciousness of mankind?" Well, that led to a rather major discovery also. The consciousness of mankind throughout the ages has been constantly, slowly, very slowly progressing. At the time of the birth of Buddha, the consciousness level of mankind was 90. At the time of the birth of Jesus Christ, the consciousness level of mankind was 100. Then down through the ages, it slowly evolved, and through the 1200s, 1400s, 1700s, it stayed at 190. It stayed at 190 century after century. It didn't move. Then suddenly in the late 1980s, at about the time of the harmonic convergence—not caused by it, but at the time of it—at the time of the collapse of monolithic communism and many other things, the consciousness level of mankind jumped from 190 to 207. Because 200 is the level of truth, 200 is the level of integrity, it is probably the most significant event, as I say, in the history of humankind, unnoticed. The shift of consciousness went from 190 to 207. That completely changes that field in which all of mankind now lives.

So how does it change it? Well, at 190, the destruction of mankind was inevitable. The destruction of mankind was quite likely, you know, the great megabomb in case Russia lost the war that was going to destroy all of mankind was a considerable likelihood. At 207 now, there's a whole new paradigm of reality. In the world in which I grew up in the 1930s, on through that century, the goal of life was success. You were supposed to make money, be successful, go to college, get a name for yourself. So the great goal of society was success. Now, at 207, we see a whole shift of paradigm. Now people are not interested in your success. I mean, you can buy some stock and be a millionaire tomorrow and so what. No. Now what we're looking at is integrity. So all the great corporations whose heads have rolled have been so because of lack of integrity. We see politicians being called to task for integrity. No. Success and monetary value and having a big car and all the stuff that used to make people happy in the '50s no longer suffices. Now people are looking. What is the integrity of this company? What is the integrity of this politician? We're looking at how truthful are they, how can they back up their statements?

So integrity is the new signal of social value. We want to invest in people and politicians and teachers who have proven integrity. Well, how can you prove it? Well, one way you can prove it is, frankly, simply by calibrating the level of it. Integrity has power. A lack of integrity can have force, monetary force for a moment, but it collapses. You can't base your life on success, and therefore, the new paradigm of value is integrity. And it's by integrity now that everyone is going to be measured, you know, how integrous as a teacher are you, how integrous as a spiritual teacher, how integrous as a university. And when you calibrate all these things, you see where integrity has sold out. We've calibrated many, many things. You can see where any compromise in integrity shows up on the dotted line. So because you can now measure it and calibrate truth from falsehood, I think we will have a new yardstick by which man will grow faster than before.

We saw for centuries it stayed at 190. No movement. From a historical viewpoint, when people say great events happened—well, great events from a perceptual viewpoint, but not from a spiritual viewpoint. Man is now in a new dimension, and 207 is critical because it only takes one feather to tip the balance from negative to positive. Every spiritual decision we make, then, tips the scale to the positive side, and that totally changes the destiny of our life. If you're out at sea, you know, a change of one degree in the compass may not seem like much, but after a couple days of sailing, you'll end up on a different continent, so one degree makes quite a bit of difference. Freedom of choice, then, spiritual choice is what we're confronted with instant by instant. We're constantly saying yes or no to choices, and those choices then determine our spiritual level and our calibrated level of consciousness and our karmic destiny.

✳ ✳ ✳

This led to my eventually becoming a spiritual teacher, right, because that's what you call me. I wanted to share my own subjective state and what I discovered and things that have never been really said before. What I teach now I call devotional nonduality. *Devotional* because one is in love with the truth, one is in love with the pathway to God through truth, and *nonduality* meaning to reach a state of enlightenment one has to transcend the ego. And the ego is dualistic in nature. Human thinking is dualistic in nature. There's an either/or, a *this* or *that*, so the spiritual student usually starts first with confronting the ego and what has traditionally been called sin and given all kinds of bad names. So the first thing I want the student to understand is the nature of the ego and to become friendly with it. And where does the ego come from? You have to get away from demonizing it. You can't see it as an enemy. The ego is nothing but animal nature. When you look at the animal kingdom, all you see is what's called the human ego. When we see it in an animal, we just say it's animal nature, but when we see it in a human, we say, "Uh-oh. Isn't that awful?" Well, no. It's not awful.

The animal brain is still active in the back of the human brain. When we became human, when we evolved, when consciousness evolved over great eons of time up through the animal world, you see very primitive life form. You see the beginning of that which is rapacious. It lives by the death of others, the reptilian world. Then you see the emergence of the mammalian, and for the first time you see the emergence of love. Love doesn't emerge on this planet for millions and billions and millions of years, not till you see the mammalian. When you actually see the the mother bird caring for the eggs and baby birds, it's really the mammalian that you begin to see. You don't see love until you see really the emergence of the maternal. Love doesn't appear until you see the mother's concern for the child, the infant, the fledgling. The paternal love, the mother has to protect the cubs from the male lion, so you don't see it arising primarily early in the evolution of the animal world.

You see the love beginning to emerge as the expression of the maternal, and then you begin to see love blossom over the ages. And, you know, romantic love, which we take for granted in today's world, is a rather recent occurrence. People didn't get married for romantic love. They got married because the family arranged it, or the kings and queens of England, for all their power, you know, weren't free to choose love. They figured marriage is one thing, love is another, so romantic love as we see it is a rather very recent and modern thing.

So anyway, when people go into spiritual work, they are always concerned about overcoming the ego. So first we say recontexualize it as the residual of the animal within us. The old animal brain is still present in the back of the human brain, and the prefrontal cortex is a rather recent emergence. If you calibrate the level of consciousness of hominids as they evolved over time, you see Cro-Magnon;

you see Neanderthal. Neanderthal calibrates around 75, at really an animal level. Although it's able to speak and talk, it's still pretty much an animal. So it's only with the emergence of the forebrain and the prefrontal cortex you begin to see ethics, morality, spiritual awareness as such.

What man, then, is trying to do is transcend domination by the animal instincts. If you take it out of the viewpoint of sin, then, and begin to see it as animal, what is an animal like? Well, you can see the human ego on display at any zoo. You go to the monkey island in the zoo, and you see territoriality. You see gangs. They hang together in groups and then fight over turf, so you see the turf wars, which is every day's headlines in the Middle East or wherever on the planet. There's always a turf war going on. And then you see the exploitation and the subjugation of the weak. You see deception and lying and camouflage, and so all you see in today's headlines is monkey island with a human expression.

Spiritual work, then, is really overcoming selfishness, self-centeredness, and egocentricity in all of its various disguises. What are the various disguises? Well, the compulsion to have, to own, to be successful, to win, and all the things that we know as egocentricity. So how does one, then, begin to transcend that? People say, "Well, I'm interested in evolving spiritually, you know. What can I do from a practical viewpoint?" Because all what you have just described can sound quite advanced and quite theoretical and quite imposing to somebody who's not familiar with the work. Actually this work becomes rather easy. The more you read it, the more you arrive at the feeling that I knew this all along. And of course, you do know it all along, but the question is, how to transform this in everyday life.

People say, "How can I grow spiritually? Do I have to go somewhere? Do I have to get a guru? Do I have to join a meditation group? Do I have to recite mantras or what?" No, you don't have to do that at all. It's so simple that it's overlooked all the time. It's a decision to be loving and kind toward all of life, including your own, at all times no matter what, to be forgiving, to be gentle, to be that which is supportive of life, so that becomes not what you do but what you are. You become that which supports life, supports all endeavors. It encourages those who need encouragement, and it becomes the energy of life itself. It becomes almost like the manifestation of the divine mother, as well as the divine father; it's the merging of the two, you see. That which is nurturing, at the same time that which is demanding of excellence, so the pathway of nonduality, then, is the devotion to spiritual principles. And as you become devoted to spiritual principles, you're brought up face to face with the mind's propensity for either/or, good or evil, liberal or conservative. You know, you're confronted constantly with so-called polarities, and to reach a very advanced state of consciousness, it is then necessary to transcend the so-called polarities of either/or-ness.

Now, *A Course in Miracles* is quite interesting because it's based on the power of forgiveness. People say, "Well, how can I forgive somebody who's so bad?" What, I remember one of the first lessons said my thoughts don't mean anything, and the minute I read that I said, "Man, this is genius. This is spiritual genius." I mean, you've got to be very, very advanced to see the truth of that. And so I just went right off, I said, "Wow, this is great. My thoughts don't mean anything," because in an advanced state, that is a fact. You know, your thoughts don't mean anything. They're occurring spontaneously, and they're not who you are anyway so they don't really mean anything. And it's obvious that any meaning that they have is any meaning you gave them, because in and of themselves they're just constructions, self-serving constructions, and don't serve any great purpose. We survive in spite of the mind, not because of it. Everybody thinks, "Well, if I stop thinking I wouldn't survive." No. If you stop thinking you would survive even better than you're surviving now, because everything is happening spontaneously.

Since that time when I was—I don't know what age it was—35 or something, whenever that profound shift of consciousness occurred, everything has been happening spontaneously of its own. The mind is automatically under the control of the spirit, and if you need to remember to take your umbrella, the mind remembers that and it's because one's survival requires that. One's survival is coming from the spirit.

* * *

In consciousness research, we discovered a lot of very interesting things, things I like to share with people because it relieves a lot of anxiety about life. We discovered, for one thing, that the human spirit doesn't enter the embryo until the third month of pregnancy, so this little potential human being is just this little embryo, and the spirit doesn't really enter it till the third month. Well, that was sort of an interesting thing that nobody had ever discovered. We also discovered that the exact moment in time of death is karmically set. From the instant you're born, the time of your leaving is already set. We also discovered that at the moment you're born, there's already a calibrated level of consciousness, and, in fact, this consciousness really changes in the human life-time much more than five points. Most people advance about five points in a lifetime. So at the very moment of birth, then, one infant calibrates at 240 and another one at 460, another one at 92, etc. In line with understanding of karma, then there must be some reason why the human spirits enter a physicality at completely different levels of consciousness.

Now, there was something interesting we learned about after you go too. We found that if you're going to be cremated or something, it's best to wait three days, that the spirit, when it leaves the body, very often needs a couple days to get used to the mourning leaving this physicality and all that's associated with it before it's ready to go on. So we found that was sort of an interesting discovery too. Wait three days. There's only one possible death that can be experienced, and as that moment arises, then if you transcend the ego, if you really got very intent on spiritual work, meditation and letting go and surrendering everything to God as it arises, as each feeling or thought arises, there's a willingness. Devotion to truth means the willingness to surrender anything and everything to God as it arises, not to cling to it, not to hang on to it, not to try and anticipate it and live on the advancing wave and not cling to the past at the back of the wave but to stay right at the crest of the wave of that which is passing through conscious experience of the existent moment.

That we're willing to surrender everything as it arises to God as it arises, to not cling to anything, and not try to reach forward to the future and not cling to the past. Eventually you begin to transcend the crest of the wave, and you begin to see that thinkingness is arising out of some base aspect of the mind. There is, like, a compulsion to think. There's like an energy of thinkingness, a desire to think. As one begins to get that thinkingness as arising of its own one begins to discern that consciousness, think-ingness, and the whole field is not your personal self. So spiritual evolution really begins to take off when you stop identifying with the physicality of the body, realize I'm not a physical body. You realize that you are not the ani-mal instincts of the ego. You begin to see that mind is happening of its own. If you were your mind, you could tell it to stop. People say, "My thoughts are driving me crazy." I say, "Well, why don't you stop them, then?" They say, "Well, I can't." I said, "Yes, it's because you're not your mind." You're not your physical body, and you're not your mind. If you were your mind, you could say stop and it would stop thinking. No. You could say, "Mind stop," and it completely ignores you. So the mind must not be who you are. If it was who you are, it would instantly obey you. No. It's got a life of its own. Wow.

So there's something that's really sort of foreign and not yourself that's running that you're paying attention to. All this thinkingness, then, is happening of its own. So we begin to really move ahead in consciousness. And people at that point very often get interested in medita-tion, and the only purpose of meditation is to sit quietly and watch how the mind is working. And as you do, you see these thoughts and these feelings arise, and if you stop resisting them and just begin to surrender them, you get to the realization that these thoughts are arising from an energy field that is devoted to the creation of thinking, of thoughts. And you begin to realize that you're hooked on them. It's really an addiction. There's really an addic-tion to this entertainment going on. So we bemoan the mind. We say, "Oh, I suffer. Oh, I wish I could forget this and forget that." That's not the truth, because if you really wanted to, you would stop. No. The thing that gives the ego its seeming hold over us is that the ego does not survive on love. It survives on *not* love. What it survives on is the juice that it gets out of its positionalities. Okay, now we're getting somewhere. You can't give up love and hate and fear and jealousy and all those things just because you decide to. You have to dismantle it. So nonduality means you start taking the mind apart to see what makes it work. Once you understand what makes it work, where its juice is coming from, then you have a chance.

So nonduality means we begin to look at thought, and we see that what propagates the endless succession of thoughts is the payoff that we get from them. You say, "Well, I don't get any payoff out of guilt and suffering." Oh yes you do. What is the payoff you get out of guilt and suffering? It's guilt and suffering. It's its own payoff. You get to feel awful. You get to feel, oh, woe is me. First of all, you get the satisfaction of egocentricity. You get to examine the wonderful, wonderful entity called *I*, with a small *i*, and its dramatic vicissitudes. The great drama of one's life plays across one's head, and one is entranced with it. What's going on is that the thoughts, the ego, creates these thoughts and feelings, and the reason they propagate is for the juice we get out of them. So you don't have to give up thinking or thoughts. The ego, all you have to give up is the juice. The juice of punishing yourself. The juice of feeling right. Think about the juice of feeling righteous.

I mean, look at victimhood. The biggest business in today's world is victimhood. It's victimhood that dominates the airwaves, dominates the courts, dominates politics. Victimhood is what it's all about, and there's enormous competition to be the bigger, better victim of the moment. To be wronged is wonderful. Nothing could happen to you better in today's world than to be wronged.

All the politicians can get up there and beat and pummel, and the trial lawyers can go, "This poor woman was walking down the street and there was an accident out in the street, and now she went and had a heart attack, so the accident in the street caused her to have a heart attack." How did the accident in the street ask this lady to have a heart attack? There's a big payoff in victimhood, friends, because that big noise out there sent her into shock, and she had a heart attack. Don't mention the fact she's been overeating for 42 years and her blood pressure is 180/120. No, just the fact there's an accident out there.

So you see the game we have of payoff. Well, that's the ego's game inside of ourselves. You get the payoff of suffering and feeling bad. You say, "That's a payoff?" Well, of course it's a payoff. If we didn't get something out of suffering, we would stop suffering. If we didn't get something out of fear, you get to be scared out of fear. You see, the ego then lives—has learned how to live—off negatives. It's like an animal who's been forced by migration to move where there's no grass and no green leaves and has now learned how to live off cactus. We have them out in Arizona. They learn how to live off the edges of cactus. So the ego then deprived of the nurturance of love has learned how to live and survive. It survives through hatred. The ego feeds on its own juice. It propagates itself, and you can see that few are the people that are willing to give it up.

If we ask what percentage of mankind is below 200, we get 85 percent. Eighty-five percent of the population on this planet is below 200, dedicated to that which is nonintegrous, and survives by virtue of dedication to that which is nonintegrous. And so all the peaceniks with all their parades and platforms, etc., and music don't change anybody's mind because whole continents feed off of and survive and live off of nonintegrity. Nothing sounds more nonsensical and sophomoric than peaceniks parading around and asking the rest of the world to commit suicide, you might say, give up the raison d'être of their whole life. Their life is about hate and getting even and revenge and feeling sorry for yourself and one-upmanship and macho in political terms, so the whole basis of survival of 85 percent of the population is nonintegrous.

Who is the audience that is reached by people who talk about world peace and all that? Well, I'll tell you who's the audience. It's people who are already there, people who already have chosen that as their lifestyle. Clap and applaud, and does that change anything? No, because those people are there already. Like the people who go to listen to classical music are already into classical music. You don't convert, you know, people that are into gangster rock to classical music by dragging them to something by Verdi. So how does the consciousness of mankind then progress?

You know, the whole continent of Africa calibrates between 40 to maybe 160 in North Africa, the Middle East, 180, 190. You're not even up to 200. We just talked about an entire continent where not one country is over 200—not one country. So that brings us back to the political realities, the reality of consciousness research and its application in everyday life, including politics and economics, is that you come out of naiveté and you begin to become aware of what it is you're talking to.

In political dialogue, then, we have to have a more reasonable understanding of who it is we're talking to. And it's embarrassing to listen to one of our politicians talk to a great politician from another country in terminology that is completely unacceptable. See, if somebody calibrates at

90 and you're talking about democracy and the vote and all that kind of stuff, you're talking about people that are starving to death for the next meal. So democracy sounds nonsensical. Then consciousness research is of great value, not only in spiritual evolution but in everyday life to make us more conscious of what is the spiritual reality of man's life in its various expressions in today's world. We saw how it evolved from the beginning of life in the hominid and then it came up through the animal kingdom, and it's advanced now and we've reached the point that there's an emergence of a new awareness that I call *Homo spiritus*. See, *Homo erectus* learned how to walk on two feet. *Homo sapiens* learned how to think with his frontal cortex. *Homo spiritus* goes beyond the intellect, calibrates at 500 and over, is aware of the field, not the content of the field, the ego and form, and the Newtonian paradigm, but is aware and experiences the power and the reality of the spiritual domain, which calibrates 500 and up.

The emergence of love, then, becomes now a more emergent, dominant field that more profoundly influences human behavior.

Dr. Hawkins ends this chapter introducing the concept of new evolved humankind as we calibrate beyond the intellect and into the greater spiritual domain of the 500s. He terms this state as Homo spiritus. *Take some time to envision what ramifications this evolutionary state might have. How would your life be different? How would Earth be transformed? Allow yourself to be guided through your imagination as you open your perception to a world of higher resonance, a more peaceful and powerful Earth.*

CHAPTER 5

The Energy *of* Life
Is Indestructible

*Fear is perhaps one of the greatest emotions that we strug-
gle with in our lives. It's the core from which many of the decisions that we make are made, perhaps more than we realize.
You may wish to begin investigating your fears.*

*Fear plays a key role in how we perceive the life cycle. The cir-
cumstances surrounding birth and death have always remained
a great mystery to most of us. We often find ourselves fighting
the fears that arise as we struggle with the unknown that shrouds
the death experience. In this chapter, Dr. Hawkins shares several provocative insights that he has gained regarding birth and
death, many of which are both surprising and reassuring.*

There's always a few things I thought every lecture should
include, and that's the answer to birth and death. Because
I don't want you worrying about it. You can quit worrying
about death forever.

The first thing we discovered is that people already
have a calibrated level of consciousness at birth. Without
karma, how would you explain then that this one's born
already 400, this one's already almost a saint, this one is
barely at 40, this one barely survives. I'm working right
now on a map of the world, and you'll see whole continents, how the consciousness level is distributed on the
whole continent. You take North America, 431. You take

Mexico, 400. You go down to South America, they're 300s. South America is all very good, the 300s, except for Haiti. All of a sudden, bang, Haiti is like 55 or something, right in the middle of the whole Western Hemisphere. Alaska, 410, Central America, they're 300s. So the Western Hemisphere is in great shape, except right in the middle of that is Haiti, calibrates at 55. You're lucky if you live to be 12 years old.

Then you flip the map to the other side of the hemisphere, and there you see Europe in the 300s. You see Russia, across the top of Russia, like 300. You look at China, 400 or so. You look at North and South Korea, in the 400s. And then you get to the Middle East and you go down to like 180—oof, 180. All of them there, 180, 140, 150. Then you get down, get into Africa, 125, then you get down to 90, 70 and even down to 40. It's like the consciousness of the humanity is like distributed almost geographically in certain areas, as though at the point of karmic manifestation as a human you come in at what you're destined to come in at. So we notice that people who already have a calibrated level of consciousness at the very moment of birth. You're born with it. Then we also discovered that at the moment of birth not only have you an assigned calibrated level of consciousness, it's not assigned, but where you've come from previous lifetimes, but the exact moment of death is already predetermined. Not the how of it. That's up to you. You can go gallantly or you can go whimpering.

You can go as a great warrior. I remember going out in lifetimes as a warrior. I was ecstatic. Above a certain level of consciousness, you remember these lifetimes, you know. It's just a conscious memory because it's all one life, you know. It's not this life and I left it. It's all one life.

But I've told people before: I'll never forget that warrior, and I, when we went out; we did it to each other, and he was fantastic. He was the best warrior around, and so was I, and we went out ecstatic. I killed him for Jesus and he killed me for Allah, and we both just broke into hysterical laughter. It was so funny.

Anyway, so the moment of death, then, can serve a certain function because unless you transcend the fear of physical death, unless you're willing to die for what you spiritually believe in, you're limited. The minute you die for what you believe in, you jump way up there. That's why the kamikaze pilot calibrates high. We all admired him. We still do, because that was World War II. If I meet a former kamikaze pilot, I feel quite honored when we bow to each other. We both did what we did for a higher purpose: loyalty to country, loyalty to God. So the exact moment of death, then, how you choose to do it, most people what they do, they make it serve some karmic purpose. Those who are smart. Get some payoff out of it, seeing as you're going to have to go through it anyway. All right. I don't want people worrying about dying. The moment of death, we have permission to ask this in front of this audience, oh, Lord, the exact moment of death is karmically determined at the very moment you're born. That's a fact. We've confirmed that over and over thousands of times. So the exact moment of death, not the how, but the when, is already set. Consequently, you don't have to worry about death. It's already handled.

You don't have to worry about living because if it's karmically set you're going to die, then somehow you have to live to get there, don't you? You're not going to die till 63, there's no point in getting worried about getting run over at 62 because you ain't leaving here till 63. People worry about all kinds of health things and all, you know, and I'll tell you, you're subject to what you hold in mind, and if you want to believe that's all right, make yourself sick with all kinds of negative beliefs, and there's a whole industry of, you know, health terrorism, and they thrive on it. And they get a secret vicious satisfaction out of watching you squirm with fear, you know what I'm saying, programming you. I'll tell you, you're not going to live any longer, so you might as well live your life and quit worrying about it.

All right, so the levels of consciousness, then, we found what I thought was false from true turned out not to be that. It turned out that consciousness, which controls the energy field of the aura and radiates down through the acupuncture system, is a very fast energy. If something is true, your arm goes strong instantly. It's a very fast response. You don't stand there and keep pushing on it for five minutes, you'll see when you do it, it's very fast. In the presence of truth, you can feel the energy of truth strengthen and flow down your arm, after you've done what we've done many times. You almost know the answer because you feel the energy of the answer coming down your arm. If it's not true, in the presence of false-hood, what the world calls falsehoods, in the absence of truth, your arm will go weak. It's impersonal. It's a pro-toplasmic response, you might say. Life recognizes that which is friendly to it.

✳ ✳ ✳

The energy of life itself is not destructible. There's the law of the conservation of energy and matter, and the law of the conservation of life is even more powerful and more dominant. You cannot kill life. You can force it from one form into another. When you swat a fly, you know the fly doesn't even notice it. It goes right on flying in its etheric body and didn't even notice. If you've been out of body—how many people have been out of body? Yeah, you hardly notice it, right? One minute you're lying in the bed; the next minute you're floating around the room. I mean, it's fantastic. Who wants to get back in there? I didn't want to get back in there. You look at the body down there, so you don't experience your own physical death. It's not possible.

The moment that life is scheduled to leave the body, it leaves the body, and you witness the dead body down there. It's an *it* there, and the *you* is here. Anybody who's gone out of body knows the you is here, that body is an it there. You don't have to worry about killing mosquitoes when you breathe in and out and all and step over everything that you might step on a gnat. Let's see. What I just said is a fact. The fly doesn't even notice that it just left its physicality. I told you, doesn't even notice it. It goes right on flying. It comes back with another body. It's like my cat. So we asked, the cat spends a lot of time dreaming when he's sleeping. He's dreaming. Does he think his dream life is real? Yes. Does he think it's more or less real than this life? No. There's this life which is fun, and then he goes back into his kitty friends and he thinks that's fun, and, you know, it's all one life. Because reality is subjective, it's not objective. The scientists would say, "Well, the kitty's real life is in your house there, and his dream life is not real." But you see how confining the intellect is. I feel sorry for scientists. I've been one.

That's what led me into the depths of hell searching for truth, because I couldn't find it in intellect. I've got enough books at home to become enlightened 23 times, yeah. Has everybody here read the entire contents of the great books of the Western world? Anybody? Well, shame on you.

I just saved you a lot of time. It ain't there. It would save me a trip into hell. That which makes you grow strong calibrates 200 or over. That which allows you to go weak is under 200; that's 85 percent of the world's population. The ultimate consciousness possible on this planet is 1,000; extremely rare. Maybe every few hundred years. Six hundred is one in 10 million people. To reach 540, which is unconditional love, 0.4 percent of the world. To reach 500, the heart chakra, to be loving, 4 percent of the world. Four percent of the population of the world is coming from the heart. Zero point four is coming from unconditional love. So we see how rare sainthood is. That's why we celebrate it. If sainthood was common, we wouldn't write books about saints. They're rare.

All right, so where is most of the world, then? You see, there's practically nobody over here at this end of the scale. Why doesn't the world just fall over that way? These numbers are logarithmic, 10 times 10 times 10 times 10 times 10, the power at the top is so enormous, it can counterbalance the entire negativity of all the world, one being at 1,000 overrules all negativity of all that is on the planet. One avatar at 1,000 counterbalances the total negativity of mankind. America calibrates 421. Our society is the 400s, the intellect, going to college, being responsible, paying your bills, decency. The 400s is reason, so we expect people to be reasonable and logical. You can see what an idiotic position that is.

I mean, folks, the Middle East lives here, and we live here. You think he's going to maintain a contract that he signs with you? Adolph Hitler signed a peace contract with the foreign minister of England at the time. That parade hit was about 185 or 190, and Hitler at the time was like 80 or something. They have no intention maintaining it because they don't live by reason and ethics. You bring home a peace treaty signed by Adolph Hitler, he fell over laughing when they walked out of that. You think we're going to keep it? What idiots. It's getting like a drug dealer, "Yeah, I owe you $20 million for this shipment of cocaine. Of course I'll have it to you Monday." You can hold your breath waiting for the check. That's what we've been doing with international relationships. You can see the lack of success over the centuries for not understanding the calibrated level of consciousness of who you're talking to. If the people we're talking to are in the 400s, they will keep the contract because in the world of reason and logic, there's law. There's contracts. All the people talk about international agreements. It's comical. International agreements with who? These people think it's a joke.

We see where the mass of humanity is, then. The average consciousness level right now is about 207. All right. So we analyzed, what was the consciousness level of mankind throughout all of time? And we, you know, if you go way back in time, Neanderthal man, you get 70. A Cro-Magnon man, *Homo erectus*, track back the evolution of consciousness through the hominid, the hominid. That's us, folks, us hominids. And you begin to see at the time of the birth of Buddha, the consciousness level of mankind was 90. The time of the birth of Jesus Christ, the consciousness level of mankind was 100. Throughout the early centuries—the 1400s, 1700s—if you go century by century by century, you'll see that the consciousness level of mankind was 190. The consciousness level of mankind continued to stay at 190 through the 1900s, the 1950s, the time of the Second World War, and finally in the late 1980s, it suddenly jumped from 190 to 207.

Let's go back to the calibrated levels. So the consciousness level at mankind then was below the level of integrity through all the centuries. It explains Ivan the Terrible, the Inquisition, the Mongol hordes coming down and slaughtering people by the millions. The Mongols didn't conquer you. They just slaughtered you. Then there was a great advance made in society called slavery. Instead of slaughtering you, they found you were good for cash. People, you see how you can contextualize it. Is it evil or is it not evil? Well, I'd rather be sold for a few bucks of gold than, on the other hand, I have one lifetime and I just assume have died, because having been a slave on a galley, I knew what it was. And in that one, I discovered that my truth was spirit, because the agony of that lifetime was so severe and to continue to stay alive meant putting up with further savagery and brutality. It suddenly came to me: they haven't got me. I can die. I left the body. Christ, I was free. I don't have to stay here and be subjected to torture. I let myself die, and I beat them. What a discovery. Wow. Wow, wow. No one can ever touch me again, you just let go and bye.

Dr. Hawkins discussed the calibration levels of mankind throughout the ages. His final words were fascinating as he took us back several hundred years and described one of his past lives as a slave who ultimately chose to die. In making that choice, he found true freedom in death.

Given the new insights that Dr. Hawkins has just shared with you, how might your perceptions change? If you knew, for example, in every cell of your being that the moment of your death is predetermined, that you no longer need to protect yourself from the clutches of death, how might your life experiences change? Again, how much do fear-based thoughts rule your life? You may wish to reflect on your current life situation and the fears that you find welling up inside of you. How much energy do those fears take from you as you focus on them throughout your day? How much power are you losing as you find yourself ruled by them? Perhaps you might choose to surrender those fears whenever they arise. Doing so will likely create greater energy and peace of mind within you.

CHAPTER 6

Gaining the Power over the Success Game

There's a cultural pull in our perceptions of success this day and age that can be challenging at times to break away from. As we go into this chapter, Dr. Hawkins shares insights on how to gain power over the success game. He illustrates how the world has shifted to a place of much greater integrity, citing the success of Sam Walton and Walmart as an example of this. As you listen, reflect on your values. Where do they lie? Do they best serve you and Earth as a whole? Are they based in fear and lack or in faith and trust?

In the late 1980s, for reasons unknown, the consciousness level of mankind went up to 207, which is incredible. Now, it doesn't sound numerically like much, but you see, we crossed the critical line. This is you're below the line and this you're above the line, and that's all the difference between life and death. So what went on at 190 was excusable, Enron included; 207, Enron's not acceptable anymore. You see how we changed. So now when I grew up, you're supposed to be successful, get through college, make money, have a new car. Success was what it was all about. The world is a solar plexus, jet, game, beer, car, more titles. It's supposed to be a recent car. I drive a Cadillac.

I grew up to own a Cadillac. That was the ultimate and I said, "I'm going to own one someday," and I do. That was the world of gain, of success, challenge, champion, win, the game of the solar plexus. The world I grew up in was the game of success, and therefore, business was one thing and church was another. Nobody mixed the two up. And in the book I think I said never trust a man in a suit and a tie, because you see, I don't wear a suit and tie, but the minute I do, watch out. So I'm going to look for a sharp deal, folks. My head switches. In the workplace, you don't mix—you're supposed to sell more peanut vending machines, and you don't tell the poor old farmer. You tell him, "Look, man, you go around, you empty your pennies out there." This guy tried to get me to sell these things when I was a kid, tell the old farmer to take your money out of the sock and put it in these peanut vending machines. You just go around there and open them up and take your money out. Of course, what you don't tell them is the peanut vending machine only empties once a year. Once a year, you're lucky, you know what I mean. If he ever gets his money back for his peanut vending machines, but that's his problem.

And I remember what the guy told me at the time. He says—and here's how it goes in business, folks—"If you don't get his money, somebody else will." Ain't that a clincher? That's enough to convince half the people in this audience. That's how integrity was sold out, and in those days, probably that was the 1930s, 1940s—I don't know when it was. Early '40s, maybe. Anyway, integrity was not what business was all about. Business was not about integrity. Walmart wasn't born yet. Two different worlds. We didn't mix business and reality, you know.

Business was the real world and then Sunday was church. Two different things.

* * *

Walmart stands as an example of integrity. Walmart, when Sam Walton was alive, was at 385, and the reason he's in *Power vs. Force* is because of his basic principles of business. I said, "Whoa, here's a guy who wants to run a business based on integrity." Walmart wasn't the biggest company in the world at that time. And so we corresponded back and forth, and I calibrated Sam and the business, and it was in the high 300s. And we made note of it in *Power vs. Force*, and of course now Walmart is the largest company in the whole world. It's not as high as when Sam was alive, because those things never are. You know, he was the radiance, but he established the principles. It's still high. It's still 365 or something. What that established is people say, "Well, business is one thing and church is another," but Sam took it in and said, "Hey, what about the old American Midwest values of get your money back if it don't work and all?"

Walmart still calibrates the highest of any big companies out there. That's why it's so powerful. Nothing else comes near it, 365. The nearest next business is like, you know, the 200s or something, and the other unfortunate thing we found. We said, "What's the average consciousness level of the CEO level of the Fortune 500 companies?" It came out at 198. Which means keep your eyes open, folks.

The interesting thing, you see, at 190 you can get away with that. At 207, you can't, because it takes an energy field quite a while before it, you know, has a profound effect on the whole ecology of our population. At 207 it doesn't work anymore, and you see the giant corporations falling. I mean, every day there's a new giant corporation that's fallen by the wayside. Another corrupt regime is being singled out by the world for straighten up, shape up, or ship out. So corrupt dictatorships, which torture their populous and steal their wealth, you know, were quite common years ago. There were only a few forms of government, and the cruel dictator was sort of classic. He still rules in parts of the world. So you can get away with it when you're below 190, but at 207 everybody begins to notice, remark about it, put pressure on it, corral human energy. So the world is changing. The world of 207 will not tolerate what it handled at 190, and we will see heads rolling down on Wall Street and internationally. I expect it will continue.

So as we get out of form, we'll see that the power goes up. This is the power. This is what guarantees that you will stay alive until you die.

The power of the Self. See, the ego would have you think that it's responsible for your survival. The ego says, "If I wasn't so clever, if I didn't remind you to take your vitamins and all, you'd be deader than a mackerel." So the downside of duality, then, is in spiritual work, it creates the illusion that there's a separate *I* that is the cause of everything, that there's a personal *I* separate from the infinite oneness of totality. The core of the ego is this egocentric, self-centered point that one assumes to be the cause. So as long as you believe in causality, then, you are stuck in a duality of a *this* causing a *that*. The pathway to enlightenment through nonduality, then, dissolves the opposites, and we'll get to that after lunch. How to get rid of a *this* causing a *that*.

At age three, there it was: existence versus nonexistence, reality versus unreality. How do you get rid of opposites? Well, I gave you the key to getting rid of the opposites this morning. *This* is not the opposite of *that*. There is no conflict between *this* and *that*, any more than there's conflict between chocolate and vanilla. So let's go to the duality of the opposites because we'll have to transcend the ego before snack time. We're going to give that ego a one-two. I told you when you gave me that expensive coffee you were in for it. Well, I live out here in the field, in the woods, and then people say, "You've got to give a lecture and talk to people." So I ring the bell, and I say, "Anybody got any espresso or something here?" Because you've got to get reenergized back into duality, or these folks will think you're out of it. Okay, chocolate versus vanilla: you can see that's an illusion. All the dualities of the world—politically, you can be enthusiastically this, but it's not necessary to hate this. You can disagree with them, but it's not necessary to hate them. Not necessary at all. It doesn't do any good, because it really brings about the opposite consequence.

The ego is built on duality. There's a *this* causing a *that*. There's a separate *I* that is the cause of *that*. And how does one transcend the polarity of the opposites? That's one of the great spiritual trusts that one has to transcend to on the way to enlightenment. The ego thinks that there's a duality between up and down, this and that, and let's see in reality what is actually going on. Let's take good and bad. Everybody says—well, everybody knows the difference between good and bad. That's a joke. If we take the duality, then, we will find that it's really not a duality. There's only one reality.

And here, with goodness, you can see goodness is either present or not present. If there's a lot of goodness, we say it's heavenly, it's sort of okay, it's not too good, it's bad, it's weak, it's horrible. You see there are the degrees of love. There's only one variable: the degree of love. Here, there's lots of love. Here, there ain't none. But they're not opposites. See, they're not opposites. It's degrees of the presence of love. There's only one variable, not two. We can do the same thing with heat.

People say hot versus cold. Hot versus cold. There's no *versus*, folks. There's just a lot of heat or not so much. And when there ain't hardly any at all, like in the snowbank, you just freeze up. There isn't hot versus cold. There's the presence of heat or the absence of heat. Okay. Value. This is something we add to a thing. This is all in our head. It's precious. It's wonderful. It's worth dying for. Take it back and get a refund; it's repulsive. That's all likeability. There's only one variable.

People say light is the opposite of dark. You see, those are just means of verbalization. There's no reality. There's no opposite of dark. There's lots and lots of light or not much of it. There's no such thing as light versus darkness. There's no such thing as evil versus good. It's a lot of something or not a lot of something. There's no opposite of rich versus poor. There's a lot of money or not so much money. All depends. Some parts of the world, I'd be considered rich. Whatever. Other parts, poor as a mouse, you know.

It all then depends on conditions, right. What we call truth, then, is always conditional, because it depends on context. There is no truth without stating what is the context. Truth, unless you state the context, cannot be defined, and that's why the great books of the Western world were never able to arrive at a definition of truth. Eventually, and this happens as you get more philosophically sophisticated. When I studied theology at a Jesuit

university, I was an atheist. And I always got a kick out of
getting a straight A's, and they got D's. They were so pious
and got D's, and I didn't believe in any of that crap and I
got an A. But I can remember seeing through the proofs of
the existence of God by Aquinas and based on Aristotle,
of course, going back to prime cause. I could see the fal-
lacy of that even intellectually, because cause—there isn't
a cause for anything. I mean, if there was, it wouldn't be of
the same class, because you'd have an endless reduction of
endless billiard balls, and there's no great billiard ball that
started the whole ball rolling.

All right. I just wanted to handle creation one more
time because when we talk about causality, then you
see how you can fall for a concept of God that suddenly
appeared, created the whole universe, and then disappeared. So we got the great throwing-of-the-dice concept
of God, who created the universe. When you think about
it, the whole thing is ridiculous. He did it in five days or
something. A day is a rotation of Earth. Earth didn't exist
yet. How are you going to do it in five days? There ain't
no Earth to rotate to give you five days. I mean, the whole
thing is ridiculous. But anyway, in essence, it's truthful.
In essence, Genesis is one of the three books of the Old
Testament that calibrate positive. It calibrates over 600
or something. And what it's really saying is out of the
unmanifest emerges the manifest as light, which is the
energy of divinity, which when it implodes upon matter
takes the form of life, that all that is manifest arises out of
that which is unmanifest.

So it is one of the books of the Old Testament that
calibrates true, because reality has no beginning or end;
because it's beyond time and dimension, then there is
no beginning or end. Because there's no beginning or

end, there's no beginning of the universe that has to be explained, nor is there any end to worry about. Beginnings and endings are not possible within reality, any more than a *now* or an *instant* is. Those are all perceptions. If you want to call now, a "now," then that was now. If you want to call *here* or *there*, then that's a moment. None of that exists within reality.

That which is always was, and it's not a matter of nowness. It's a matter of alwaysness. It's not possible within reality for a creator to come in existence, create the universe, disappear, then on judgment day, "Hi, how did things go?"

Rolls the dice, and then, chicken-like, disappears. Hiding. Now he's cowering up there when you get there. Yeah. The great judgment day. Because one's karma is a continuous ongoingness. You see, there's no discontinuity even possible in the universe. One's karmic propensity then is constant, constantly by every choice, so let's settle when judgment day is.

Judgment day is every day, continuous, ongoing, inescapable. It's the absoluteness of the justice of divinity. The infinite field, then, of divinity, like a giant electromagnetic field, and you're like a little iron filing in the field. What you are, what you decide, determines where you are in the field every second, does it not? You are already at the subject of infinite judgment right now. You don't have to wait for tomorrow for judgment. Today is already the result of the judgment of where your reality is in the infinite space of divinity. So who you are is who you are continuously. Therefore, the justice of divinity is absolute. Consequently, we're all safe. Thank you.

Dr. Hawkins certainly has challenged prevailing concepts on the creation of the universe, karma, and judgment day. If there is no cause to existence on Earth and time is an illusion, much of what we fear is not based in any reality. You might ask yourself, then, how much energy you expend concerning yourself with the outcomes of mistruths. Remember, a change in your perception can happen in an instant. The choice is yours.

CHAPTER 7

War Is the Absence *of* Peace

* ✳ *

As Dr. Hawkins expands on the concept of war and peace, you might ask yourself what wars you are currently creating in your life. Do you believe that you can choose peace? How might things change if you did? Are you suffering from an inner war within yourself? Remember that peace is always there, ready to be fully embraced.

People think war and peace are opposites. They are not opposites at all. People think because nobody's getting shot, you have peace. You don't have peace, because that which lives off war is very alive. In fact, it has peace demonstrations. The reason I don't go to peace demonstrations is they're too dangerous. They've got dogs, police, water hoses, people with face masks, clubs. No, thanks. Peace is the natural state when truth prevails. It's the field. See, the field itself, the natural state is peace; when truth prevails, you automatically have peace. War has nothing to do with violence. It has to do with the automatic condition when falsehood prevails. The opposite of war is not peace. Therefore, the basis of war, if it's falsehood, would be ignorance, the inability to tell truth from falsehood.

So the stunning thing about *Power vs. Force*—and I can say that because there's no *me* to feel egotistical about it; I was the witness to the writing of *Power vs. Force*—was that it discerned for the first time in all of human history how to tell truth from falsehood. The karma of mankind changed with the writing of that book. Until that point, nobody in time could tell the difference between truth and falsehood except an advanced mystic.

The basis of war, then, is ignorance. When you watch the history on the History Channel and how Hitler youth grew up, it breaks your heart because they thought they were going to Boy Scout camp. They had fires and they held hands and they did brave things for their fatherland. You can see the innocence. So the human mind is incapable of telling truth from falsehood because it's only hardware, and what society puts in is software. The hardware is unchanged. *A Course in Miracles* says innocence is untarnished, no matter what. The hardware is not affected by the software. Society puts in the software, so you can take these innocent children, when you look at the Hitler youth in the '30s, their innocence, their pride in country, their devotion to their fatherland, to their duty, was incredible. They're like all little Eagle Scouts, right, led to slaughter. In the last century, 100 million people have died because of that innocence—100 million.

The condition, then—the Buddha said there's only one problem, and Jesus Christ said there's only one problem: ignorance. "Forgive them, they know now what they do." Ignorance. Buddha said there is only one sin: ignorance. Human consciousness had not evolved to the point that it earned sufficient karma to learn the difference between truth and falsehood, so the best they could say was "by their fruits you shall know them." Ten thousand slaughtered civilians, I suppose, would be the fruits by which you should know them. The bombing of civilians would be, I suppose, suspicious, that this guy ain't all right up there. But not for everybody. There was no dearth of people willing to go and champion this guy. Humankind cannot discern truth from falsehood. Consequently, it cannot discern a leader from a megalomaniac.

The book I'm writing now has quite an extensive chapter on megalomania. The world doesn't know a megalomaniac from a leader, doesn't know a Jesus Christ from a Hitler. So the German people worshiped the führer instead of God. The egomaniac, then, takes the place of God, and the people worship the egomaniac. The people that are worshiped, the great leaders, calibrate all below 100—Stalin, Hitler.

The consequences are the ego becomes programmed into polarized ego positions. It cannot tell truth from falsehood. Joseph Goebbels said if you repeat a lie often enough, everybody will believe it. It turned out to be so. Every politician knows that—otherwise they'd never get elected. Programming people's egos into ego positions is easy because all you need is a distortion of truth. Man for the first time really has within his society now the power to survive. At 190, it was eventually the ultimate atomic bomb, which the Russians were planning, and would have happened in case they lost the war. The great bomb that would destroy all of life on the planet was a certainty, because that which is below 200 has devoted all of its energies to destruction, and the destruction of all of human life is its ultimate glee, to kill everybody. Wouldn't that make an egomaniac happy? That's why we can't deal diplomatically and politically with people who think that way. We can't even conceive of that.

If we calibrate various wars, we see the position of truth versus falsehood, and you see what the consequence was to mankind. So you can take all of history, take everything—we even got a Napoleon at the bottom. So you calibrate the positions of all the people, the positions of all the politicians, the positions of the countries, the positions of the elements that are operating to bring about the consequences, and now once you see how the game board is set up, the solution is obvious. The reason you can't succeed is you don't know how the game board is set up unless you can calibrate the levels of truth. Before World War II, the prime minister of England, Neville Chamberlain, signed a peace treaty with Hitler. Chamberlain was about 180 or 190, and Hitler was about 78 at the time. Now, are you surprised that the peace agreement between the guy who's 180 and a guy who's 78 didn't last? That's real integrity for you. So Britain had to replace Chamberlain with Winston Churchill to save them all, because he was at 510.

I thought just for fun we'd do the Duke of Wellington versus Napoleon. The Duke of Wellington was 405, and Napoleon was 75.

Churchill and Theodore Roosevelt were the energy of integrity that says we will fight to the end. Then some people switched in the middle of the whole thing, and this guy went from this side to this side. He spilled the secrets of Los Alamos, and so then people that you would think maybe are suspect like Heisenberg and Wernher von Braun were integrous people. You see, General Rommel was 203. Kamikaze pilots were 390, very dedicated people. The Luftwaffe was honorable. Hirohito was right on the edge, 200. Yamamoto was doing his duty for his country. You see how interesting all that is. Then you see the consequences over here. The League of Nations was too weak to prevent the war. One eighty-five hasn't got the you-know-whats to make it happen. The attack on Pearl Harbor was 45. Goebbels was 60. This was the guy that sold the youth a lie.

So down here you see the worst of all the people, and I thought I'd put in there for fun: Lord Haw-Haw. There was Lord Haw-Haw and Tokyo Rose; both were propagandists at the time. Lord Haw-Haw was a British turncoat, and he would broadcast anti-English propaganda for the Germans. Okay, so that just shows you how we can analyze a political situation, all the people involved. You don't have to blow each other up to see how the game is going to work. What you have to do is diagnose it correctly.

It was inspiring to learn how Sir Winston Churchill calibrated at the level of 510 and single-handedly saved the world from further destruction in World War II. As Dr. Hawkins progresses, it becomes crystal clear that the power of one individual who resonates at a higher level of consciousness can have much greater impact on the world than thousands calibrating at lower levels. What might this mean to you, then? Again, going back to choice, in every moment of every day, we each have a choice to live in power or live in force. Love, compassion, and grace must begin as a flame that we light within ourselves. Making the choice to fully embrace and love ourselves first and foremost and then carrying that compassion beyond ourselves and into the world is integral in this work.

Take a moment to reflect on your current judgments. What are you punishing yourself for in your life? Where do you most judge yourself and others? Remember you can always choose differently. Now take some time to credit yourself for the instances when you have chosen power over force. Think back to situations where you felt you were in your authentic power. Feel into that experience and be willing to acknowledge yourself for the powerful choices that you've made. You have just taken further steps along your path of spiritual enlightenment.

CHAPTER 8

Surrendering to the Silence

* ✳ *

According to the Buddhist parable, enlightenment will come with ease once you truly want it. One of the fundamental ways to reach this state is to learn the art of surrender. When one surrenders every aspect of themselves to the divine—their suffering and joys, their challenges and victories, their love and hatred, their courage and their fears—then their lives become transformed.

As Dr. Hawkins opens this chapter, he delves into the world of greater enlightenment, the divine states. As one calibrates at 600 or above, they have discerned the illusion of the ego. He further clarifies what the ego actually is and our relationship to it, knowing that the remedy lies in the silence that is always present beyond the noise of the ego mind. Surrendering to the silence awakens us to a world that is far beyond the limited realm that we have created for ourselves.

I wanted to mention the usefulness of the capacity to tell truth from falsehood and why mankind now really has a chance to survive—not just exist on a day-to-day basis but actually survive in some kind of spiritual integrity. You have to first know what the facts are, so we tried to supply how you arrive at the facts. Truth, then, requires an objectivity that the ego is not capable of. This bypasses the ego and its belief systems, and gives us just a number.

The number is impersonal. It doesn't care who wins the election. We can calibrate chocolate and vanilla. Therefore, it has a pragmatic usefulness. Now, people wanted to know how to transcend the ego, so we tried to show that the ego is based on the assumption of causality. There is a *this* causing a *that*. It then builds its structure based on the polarity of the opposites: heat versus cold, good versus bad, etc.

The ego, then, is a whole structure and superstructure of positionalities. To transcend the ego means to undo its positionalities. The Map of Consciousness®, which has gotten to be quite well known, goes up to 600, and at 600 is enlightenment, and then it just says the level from 600 on up are the enlightened and divine states. If you want to calibrate the truth of spiritual realities, I'll save you the work of going through this with kinesiology. You will see that these time-honored titles refer to spiritual energies that are definable. They're not just somebody's fantasy. You know, is God a fantasy? And the atheist says it's a fantasy, but we can demonstrate that power of the godhead is infinite, as divinity and creator are infinite. And archangels calibrate at 50,000 and over—we're talking about logarithm. Ten times ten, fifty thousand times. A lot of voltage.

In the depths of hell, the entity within cried out, "If there is a God, can you help me?" The passing thought of an archangel is all it took. There must have been an archangel cruising by, heard the prayer. What the world calls an avatar, then, is 985. All I wanted to demonstrate is that they are also definable and calibrate-able. In ordinary consciousness, the ego identifies and says, "This is reality, this is the *I*, this is the me," and as one progresses spiritually, what happens is this begins to diminish as the focus and the intensity, the egocentricity, then, the definition of self begins to change. It's as though it dissolves in the sea. So there's no war. There's no conflict. The only thing I don't like about *A Course in Miracles*—I think the workbook is correct. I think the textbook has an error in that it sort of sets up the ego as a foe, and you get polarized with the ego. So I think the textbook came from a different source than the workbook, frankly. The workbook I think is correct.

You don't want to get polarized. The ego is not your enemy. It's just an illusion of who one thinks one is, and this illusion is based on a dualistic structure of the ego, which tends to make you think there's an *I*, a *this* that causes a *that*. That's where I say if you let go of the illusion, then things come about as a result of causality. You will save yourself 42 lifetimes. Forty-two, I never heard that one before.

How does one transcend this identification with the ego? First of all, merely to hear the truth already has an impact, whether you know it or not. The consciousness of everyone in the room has already jumped just to have heard it. The Buddha said to have even heard of enlighten-ment, you will never be satisfied with anything less, never; through all your lifetimes, you have heard it. Everyone in this room has heard it, or they wouldn't be here. It's the future that's creating your present. You think it's your past that is propelling yourself from the past, that you're being pushed by your past. No, you're being sucked into your future.

You're being pulled by destiny, because by an act of the will you have already chosen your destiny, and now this is the unfolding of what is required to reach it. That's all. Therefore, there's no point to complaining about it, unless you want to. Do not feel guilty about complaining.

How does one transcend this ego? First of all, there is no such thing as the ego. There's only the tendency of these energies to form a structure. There's only a tendency. They can be easily undone. There's two ways, meditation and contemplation—and prayer, of course. And devotion. Be one with the field. So if you are aware primarily of the field, see, the obsessive-compulsive gets caught up in this thing here, and it drives you crazy. He's got to know every little detail here, which is totally irrelevant. You know what I'm saying? Was your lunch $1.32 or $1.37? I don't know. Who cares? I tell the IRS it's two bucks, you know what I mean? I save them all that bookkeeping. I include the tip. Tip doesn't show up on the receipt, so if I save the receipt, it won't do me any good because it doesn't include the tip.

Anyway, they live here and drive you crazy with all their focus on detail. So the *I*, the sense of Self, then, this is the vision of the totality. You live in the infinite space in which everything is happening. To be focused on, you might say peripheral vision rather than central vision, is to be aware of the totality of the situation. The entirety of all of us being here and the energy of us being here and what that means for what should be said here and what should be heard, speaks of its own. Sure, there's individual questions, but that's not going to be what this whole afternoon is about. It's about the totality of the energy and the totality of these beings and their collective drive. That's what it's all about.

So if you move around in a peripheral world, you're always focused on the totality of the situation. Unfortunately, you miss a lot of the details. It's best to be married; if you do this, who tells you that you put the shirt on with the hole in the sleeve? *Oh jeez,* I thought, *she'll never see that.* It's my favorite shirt. In her world, you cannot wear a shirt if it has a hole in it. In my world, nobody notices it.

I pay attention to the field all the time. You can do the same thing in meditation, where you're constantly aware of consciousness itself. The opposite way is to focus on the content. There is another form of meditation or contemplation in which there is an absolute fixity of focus on the immediate present as it arises with no selection, intensely focused on the head of a pin, constantly. You're focused on this as you say this. You're focused on the exact words you're saying. You're focused on the exact instant. So you're staying intensely focused in the intense now, what the world calls now peripheral and central vision. The retina is sort of set up that way, too, with your focus with the macula or the field. The willingness to surrender all to God—so devotional nonduality means the love for God is enough that you're willing to surrender everything that stands in the way of the realization of the presence of divinity, which turns out not to be an "other" but the Self. You thought it was going to be out there later. It's the source of one's existence, to come to the realization the radical reality of subjectivity. We take subjectivity for granted. We take the field for granted. We take consciousness for granted. This is what we take for granted. This is what we think is important. This is what's trivial and irrelevant, and this is what you are. We ignore what we are and return to focusing on that which we are not.

At this very instant, 99 percent of your mind is silent. The reason you don't notice it is because you're focused on the 1 percent that's noisy. It's like you have a vast amphitheater—let's take a great ballpark that seats 400,000 people. Nobody's there in the middle of the night, but over in the corner, there's one little tiny transistor radio or one little four-inch TV. That's what you're focused on. The whole amphitheater is empty. There's nobody in the seats. But you think this is where the action is, so you're focused on the little tiny thing of the moment attracting your attention. Because attention is focused here, you think that's what your mind is. That's not what your mind is. The mind is the absolute silence. If your mind wasn't silent, you wouldn't know what you're thinking about. If it wasn't for the silence in the woods, you couldn't hear any noise. How could you hear a bird sing? It's only against the background of silence. It's only against the background of the innate silence of the mind that you can witness what the mind is thinking about.

At that realization, you call it *it* instead of *me*. It's not what my mind is thinking about. It's what it's thinking about. That same realization comes about with the body, when you leave the identification with the body. You see it doing what it's doing. I have nothing to do with it, never did have anything to do with it. It belongs to nature, and it's karmically propelled. It just does what it's going to do. It's as entertaining to me as anybody else. I mean, it's just a novelty.

So what are those fields of realization? I want to get to that. As things arise, then, there's a willingness to surrender them to God. There's a willingness to surrender everything as it arises. You see, when you hear a musical note, the note arises and then it falls. As you hear the note, it's already crested and it's already falling. So surrender, then, is the willingness to let go all positionalities of everything that arises as it arises, not to label anything, not to call it anything, not to take a position about it. The willingness to surrender to everything as it arises will allow you to go through major surgery without anesthesia. I've done it several times. The minute you resist the pain or call it pain, the minute you say, "They're cutting my thumb off," the minute you start to resist the pain, the pain is excruciating. The minute you get off your position but you stay on the edge of the knife, let go of resisting. Let go of resisting. You can disappear any illness as it arises.

So if you fall down and you feel you've just twisted your ankle, you can't call it pain. You can't call it twisting an ankle. There are sensations coming up. You look over, you're resisting the sensations. Don't label them anything. You're not experiencing pain. Nobody can experience pain. Pain is a label. You can't experience diabetes. You can't experience pneumonia. You can't experience any of those things. Those are all words, labels. You can cough. You can't even experience a cough. That's another word you put on it. There's a sensation. You let go of resisting the sensation, completely surrender it to God, the willingness to surrender everything to God as it arises. So as it arises, the willingness to surrender it brings you into a state of alwaysness, of the presence of reality as the source of existence. If you live on the front of the wave, you're always anticipating the future. The ego is always trying to be one up on the next moment. If you surrender it late, hang on to it a while. You're always living in the past. Why did I say that? Why did I do that? So this one lives in fear. This one lives in regret. Neither one's reality, trying to get one up on the future. Because you're not there yet, you can't get one up on the future because when you get there, you'll have created a new future that you can never get one up on. The future's always out there.

As Dr. Hawkins ends his chapter, he leaves us with a challenge to let go of resisting any sensations that we have as they arise. By letting go of resisting and surrendering everything to God, you will find yourself in what he terms the alwaysness. Are you currently surrendering any aspects of your life to the divine? Perhaps for the next several days you might create the intention to start the surrendering process. You may find that the simple act of offering your experience and feelings up to the divine as they arise will free you from the burdens that you carry as you attempt to solve all of life's challenges on your own.

CHAPTER 9

Seeing the Innocence *of* Human Consciousness

Are you ready to make a change in your life? Take some time each day to sit quietly and see what comes of it. If you meet with resistance, you may wish to explore what that resistant self is trying to tell you. Then simply surrender that resistance up to the divine.

As Dr. Hawkins will point out, we also need to surrender how we see things so that we can transform how we experience life. The surrender starts with choosing to see the innocence that is at the core of human consciousness. When we open the door to that innocence and perceive life not from a place of condemnation but from a place of compassion, we experience a major shift in our personal world and in the world at large.

The willingness to surrender how you see things then begins to transform how you see and experience life. Instead of being angry and condemning, you see that people cannot help being the way they are. So we're saying here's these teenagers throwing rocks at each other and provoking the police into attacking them, and you begin to see they can't help themselves. And so as you really go into great depth, you begin to discern the basic innocence of human consciousness. The consciousness itself is like the hardware of a computer, and the ego is like the software. The consciousness itself is unable to tell truth from falsehood. It cannot tell whether it's being programmed, like the Nazis did with the Nazi youth, into falsehood or whether it's truth. So then we understand why Christ and Buddha said, "Forgive them for they know not what they do." The hardware of the computer is unaltered by the software. The consciousness of the youth is innocent.

So those kids who shoot Americans, let's say for Allah, then, are looked at with compassion. You can see that they have been abused, so you see the spiritual abuse of the ignorant. And because of the innocence of human consciousness, its inability to discern truth from falsehood, mankind is led down the path of falsehood. If you look at the History Channel, you know, the history of the Nazi movement in the '30s, etc., and you see the young people in Germany, patriotic. It's like going to Boy Scout camp. They're around the campfire singing songs and hiking and doing all this for their country, for their fatherland, for the führer. You say, "How could they have believed anything other than that?" If I'd been there, I would have been doing the same thing. You see the innocence. So we begin to see the basic innocence of human consciousness, and now it allows us to forgive everyone. You see that everyone is being run by the programs with which they've been programmed. I mean, what else could they think? People believe the media because television comes across so fast, they've already believed it before they've had a chance to even examine or question it.

So the mind gets programmed, and so you see on the one hand the ego survives by juicing negativity. On the other hand, you can't help but do that. It can't help but be that which it is. And without the power of spiritual truth, frankly, it's unable to transcend itself. The value of spiritual truth is that without it, nobody would transcend the ego. It's because of the great avatars, it's because of the great power of spiritual truth and those who have realized the reality in their lives and is the source of their own existence, that creates the power of the field, and the power of the field is where people derive inspiration to then transcend the limitations that they find themselves at.

When we understand, then, that basically human consciousness is innocent, it doesn't know truth from falsehood—so the reason I had to write the book *Power vs. Force* is because it staggered me, and I realized man has never had a chance to know truth from falsehood. The best man has been able to do is to follow the intellect and end up at a consciousness level of 460, which leaves you stuck right in the middle of the mind and its dualities. And therefore war and hatred and all are destined to go on and on, because without spiritual energy and truth to transcend it, the mind is hopelessly caught in its own web.

And it gets paid off for getting—so as it goes round and round and ruminates, it gets a payoff. Therefore, it's self-propagating. The ego, unaided without external spiritual truth, will forever go around and around, chasing its own tail. Each person as they do what they think is personal spiritual work is actually influencing the entire field. So the prevailing level of consciousness of mankind then progresses as a consequence of the collective spiritual effort of all of us. Every choice, every spiritual decision we make, reverberates around the universe. It says in scripture not one hair of your head goes uncounted, and we discovered with kinesiology that that is a fact. Anything anybody's ever done, thought, felt—every decision that's ever been made is recorded forever in the field of consciousness.

People who say they don't believe in karma can do so as a belief system, but they would still have to explain how is it that all phenomena that have ever occurred throughout all of history are recorded forever. How do you explain that every entity that gets born on this planet already has a calibrated level of consciousness? Therefore, they did not arise out of nothingness, but out of somethingness, and what is that somethingness out of which we all arise and to which we all return? That takes us out of the limitation of the timeframe of the present, and we begin to see and experience life in a greater dimension. And the spiritual realities that arise out of contemplating such things then sort of encourage our investigation into spiritual truth, which is the purpose of this kind of work.

I wanted to first present the whole panorama of consciousness. It's evolution. It's quality. It's nature. How it's been approached from science, reason, logic, philosophy, ethics, theology, and religion, how it has evolved in mankind, how it manifests itself and the part that it plays in everyday life for us then requires energy, and it exhausts people. So people can only exert force to a certain point, and then they begin to collapse.

Power, on the other hand, does not exhaust itself. In fact, the more it's used, the more powerful it seems to be. For instance, if we experiment with forgiving people and being willing to love unconditionally, we find that that capacity grows. In the beginning, it may seem difficult to love that which seems unlovable, but if we dedicate ourselves to being that way in the world, then we find that it's easier and easier. We find that with force, the more you give away, the less you have. But with power, the more you give, the more you have.

So the more loving a person is, the more loving their world becomes, and we begin to experience the world of our own creation, you might say. Some people say, "You go to New York City, they're all so cold and horrible there. I hate New York City, and they're all mean." Another person goes to New York City and says, "My goodness, it was the most wonderful people. All the waitresses were neat and the cab drivers were—it's just an incredible place." Well, it's because in the presence of love we, you know, precipitate the emergence of love in other people, and when we're not loving, we tend to bring forth the negative side of their natures. So all we're experiencing, then, is the kind of world that we're precipitating by virtue of what we ourselves have become.

* * *

The contrast between power and force is given dramatically by a historical example of the British Empire, or vis-à-vis Mahatma Gandhi. Well, Mahatma Gandhi, as you know, was an acetic, Hindu acetic, and if you calibrate Gandhi, he's over 700. At the time that he confronted the British Empire, the British Empire was the greatest force the world had ever seen. It ruled one-quarter of the world, a third of the planet, and the seas, so it was the greatest force the world had ever seen. And when I grew up, the British Empire was still the great British Empire upon which the sun never set.

Well, against that stood a little 90-pound Hindu Indian, skin and bones. He stood up to the British Empire, stood up to the lion. So here's this 90-pound acetic who then confronts the great lion that ruled one-third of the planet. The interesting thing is that Mahatma Gandhi, by doing nothing—in fact just saying he's going to stop eating, and if they didn't like it, he'd just starve to death—threw the world into a panic. And at 700, Gandhi stood there—well, 700 is, of course, enormous power, extremely rare on the planet—and faced off the British Empire, which in its pridefulness and self-interest calibrated at 190, and without firing one single shot he defeated the entire British Empire and took it apart and brought the end of colonialism, which was followed by other nations, then, who also one after another, gave up their colonialism. So it was not only the British Empire but colonialism per se that he defeated, and self-rule became the dominant political system in the world today.

So what Gandhi really represents, then, just like AA, the 12-step movements, all spiritual groups around the world, is they demonstrate the influence of power. Power doesn't cause things. Force can be said to cause things within the Newtonian paradigm. Power influences things. Now, you know that a quark is going to rise depending on the density of the medium that it finds itself, so by prayer, by spiritual evolution, what happens then is that mankind creates a very powerful field, this field of spiritual reality, which then begins to lift and affect all of mankind. It affects the whole paradigm of reality and values. So as we mentioned before, integrity is now becoming a predominant value in our society. It's being talked about constantly in the media. So we have a whole new value system.

Now, that was not brought about by the mechanism of force. Nobody forced the news or the media to begin valuing integrity, but integrity as a social value I'm speaking of—not as a spiritual value, but as a social value. So we all live by our own principles. Spiritual growth then means what principles do we live by, and as we grow and mature, we choose different principles. You know, some people live by the principle of always be right, never give the sucker a break. People come out and state what their principles are. Sometimes they seem quite outlandish, but you can say they're integrous to the degree that they live by them. They are living by what they're committed to. So I respect what people say they're committed to, and I think to the degree they live by that, then they're being virtuous by their own definition.

So calibrated level of consciousness, to some degree, then, reflects the degree to which we live by our own stated spiritual choice. You might say karma or spiritual destiny, but a calibrated level of consciousness, then, is a consequence of spiritual freedom of choice. So we have freedom of choice at every moment, but this freedom of choice seems to be obscure. We seem to be run by programs, and one reason that we try to transcend the ego is because we don't want to be at the effect of the ego. We would like the mind to stop long enough for us to deliberate and make a choice. And so often we do a thing quickly and we regret it later, and you sort of get a resentment: "Gee, I didn't have a moment to really think about that." Our spiritual choices then tend to determine which way we choose when the moment arises. If it wasn't for the silence of consciousness, you would not be able to know what you're thinking. It's because of the silence of the force that you can hear sound. It's because the mind is silent you can hear or see or picture what you're thinking.

Therefore, the content of the mind must be going on in the space of no mind, which is a classical term meaning thoughtless, formless consciousness upon which thoughts reflect themselves. So we withdraw our investment and preoccupation and identification with the content of thinking and begin to see that we're the space in which thinking can occur. So the value of meditation, then, is it focuses us so that we withdraw our investment in identification with the content of thought to the space in which the thought is occurring, and we begin to see that there is a witness to the thinking. There is an awareness to the witness, and that there's a substrate that underlies all of it that is beyond time, beyond dimension, and that is independent of personal identification. And the identification, then, with consciousness itself lifts us out of the identification of our reality as either the body or the mind or the thoughts or the feelings and takes us to a greater dimension.

As we move into that greater dimension, then, we confirm that spiritual reality that underlies our existence. People become involved in spiritual work on a practical level. They want to know: How can I forgive my enemies when I hate them so much after all they've done to me? How can I feel hope when I'm really depressed? How can I get rid of fear when I'm scared all the time? So it starts out on a very practical—many people start out on a very practical, nitty-gritty level. Other people start out from a different level. They start out through inspiration. They will hear an inspirational speaker and get uplifted, so one can start from curiosity. One can start from sort of a spontaneous evolution within one's own consciousness. I think spiritually evolved people inspire others outside of their awareness. Because they influence the field, people that ordinarily would not be interested in spirituality suddenly become curious, not through any inner prompting, but as a consequence of the field.

So if you're around people who are more spiritually evolved, one finds one's own interest in it spontaneously becoming more intense, not through any deliberate decision making but just because it's more interesting, the same as if you're around people that are into sports. You tend to listen to it more and be more interested in it. We hear all the time clinically, you know, people have some kind of disaster in their life, an illness or drugs or alcohol or criminality or grief or loss and what can they do about it. The willingness to surrender life to God, of course, is one of the most profound spiritual tools. So people ask which spiritual tools are the most powerful. I always say humility, the willingness to surrender life, to let go wanting to control it, to let go wanting to change it, the willingness to surrender how you see things to God, then, or to some higher spiritual principle, because God is not a reality. It's just a word to most people, a hoped-for reality but not an experiential reality to most people, until they become more spiritually advanced and begin to experience the presence of the field itself and intuit its enormous power.

And then they reverence God because they respect the infinite power that they begin to intuit. So what we can do on a practical level, then, is become the best person we can become. I'd say to become kind toward all of life in all of its expressions, no matter what. And that includes one's self, to be willing to forgive one's self, to see the limitation of human consciousness. I always feel that the more educated you are about the quality of consciousness, the nature of consciousness, the easier it is to follow spiritual principles. If you understand that human consciousness is intrinsically innocent and cannot control that which it's programmed by because it can't tell truth from falsehood, you begin to feel compassion automatically. So I feel—one reason I like to lecture is because certain pieces of information are already transformational. You don't have to sit down and sit cross-legged and do mantras and meditate for hours at a time or go to an ashram. Once you understand the intrinsic innocence of human consciousness, you instantly are able to forgive people.

So I've been impressed by the power of spiritual truth conveying information. That's why I do the research and that's why I write and talk about it; it's because to merely to have heard it already changes how you feel and see it altogether already. If the human being can't tell truth from falsehood, how can you fault it or kill it for being false? You can feel sorry for it. So now instantly you understand what the Buddha said—there's only one sin and that's ignorance—which is the same thing that Jesus said, and which Krishna said, though Krishna said, "Those who reverence me, even though they're totally mistaken and wandering in the wrong direction, belong to me; they are mine." In the end run, then, man is forgiven because of his profound ignorance, and if he knew better, he would do better. He can't do better until he knows better, so the evolution of consciousness is then the means by which man learns to know better.

It's only when suffering reaches certain levels or one's spiritual awareness, because of the presence of the spiritual truth of others around, begins to dominate, that one begins to choose. So the way situations like that evolve is because the people themselves learn through the misery of that experience that they have to choose a different way. Without the horror and the suffering of certain kinds of human dilemmas, nobody turns to God. It's called hitting bottom. So when a society hits bottom—when the Middle East has had it with enough agony, when enough busloads of children blow up on both sides, when enough young people are mowed down by machine guns—suddenly somebody gets the bright idea maybe this isn't the way. Then society turns around. But it hasn't earned the karmic right to turn around until it does so, until you actually turn to God and ask God for help.

So you might say not having earned it, they have not benefited by peace because they don't want peace. We want peace for them. It's like us wanting to get somebody else sober. Well, we tell people to go to Al-Anon. The first step in that program is to look at wanting to control others. So we can't try to control people and change them because we have the bright idea of how we would like it to be for them. No. What we can do is pray for them and hold in mind a different way of looking at things. Wow. So if somebody's lying in bed at night and they're dismayed with the way the world is going and the way their life is going and the way their country is going, and suddenly they get an inkling out of nowhere of how it could be, then there's the beginning of the light, which symbolizes the spread of the spirit. So the spread of the spirit, then, is the only hope in salvation. For spiritual evolution to occur, there has to be a willingness on our part—let's say a willingness to see the innocence of others.

Dr. Hawkins clearly shifts the paradigm that many of us find ourselves in. We seek to control others in the world as a whole by trying to fix them. He speaks of society's hitting bottom, explaining that, like an alcoholic, only the society itself can make changes. Explore this new truth. If all of your external efforts to transform the world prove to be in vain, then focusing your efforts specifically on your own life frees your energy to flow as the divine would have it.

Next time you feel yourself trying to control or fix anyone or anything, take a moment and perhaps ask yourself what it is that you fear. Gaining clarity and then choosing different intentions are key steps in the surrender process.

CHAPTER 10

Experiencing beyond the Phantasmagoria

What are the bare essentials that you could not do without in your life? Perhaps you'd like to make a list of them and then make a list of all the nonessentials that are currently encumbering your life. As you strip your life down to the simplest essentials, you begin to gain further clarity on the paradigms that shape your life and the inner workings of the ego. With time and discipline, you learn to let go of the ego's propensities, just as you were able to let go, one by one, of the nonessentials in your life. The outer world reflects the inner workings.

In this chapter, Dr. Hawkins provides even more detail on the payoffs of the ego. He explains that the decision is yours either to love God or to struggle in the ego-based emotions of shame, guilt, fear, revenge, and hatred.

So, how can you let go of these propensities of the ego to hang out with ego's shame and guilt? Why does the ego hang out with shame, guilt, fear, all that stuff—with greed, with desire, with lust, with hatred? Why? Because it gets a payoff. The ego mulches negativity, and it gets juice out of it. The ego survives by virtue of the juice it gets. Now, if you don't believe it, you watch any nightly TV of the conflict in the near East. Let's take Palestine and

Israel. They're the best example. They're on every night. This side throws rocks at this side. This one hits one with the fire hoses. This one hits them back again. They love it. They've been at it for centuries. It's a game. Look at the face on them. They're alive with hatred. Take that, you son of a bitch. Die.

Man, they're so hyped up. Don't you see how they're pumped up by it, how they thrive on it? Don't you see how peace is the last thing they want? All you got to do is have a new peace negotiation and the bombs start again. Every peace negotiation means another busload of kids goes up. I hate it when the peace negotiation comes up. Everyone's good for at least one busload of kids. Everyone. They want peace like a hole in the head. They're devoted to war, to hatred. The ego thrives off of it. If they had peace, who would all these warriors be? They'd be nobody. Stupid has-beens. Nobodies.

All right. The willingness to surrender the payoff of the ego, then, allows you to let everything go experientially as it arises. The willingness to let go of the payoff of grief, anger, resentment, hatred. So what do you surrender to God in the way of surrender? What does devotion mean? I love thee, oh, Lord, greater than I love the glee I get out of my hatreds, my wickednesses, my shame, my guilt, my revenge. Either you love God or you love revenge. You can't have them both. You either love God or you love self-pity. So it's always really a choice. Am I willing to surrender this for the love of God or not? To become enlightened, that power has to be powerful. You have to be willing to give up everything for God—everything—because at the last moment before that ultimate experience reveals itself or condition takes over, rather, you will be asked to surrender your life, the core of what you think is your life,

the core of the ego, the self, the real you for the last ump-
teen lifetimes. You've got to lay that down for God. It's
scary, because you've let go of this payoff. You look at all
the stuff, and now suddenly there's like an infinite presence that is like yourself, what you think is your self, and
this, too, one lays down. And there's a moment of terror,
and you experience death, one and only death. You never
experience it again. You've never experienced it before,
and you'll never experience it again, but there is one death
you live through. You don't know that you're going to live
through it.

The ego has the notion that it's going to be the same,
only be enlightened. I'll still be me but I'll be an enlightened me. No. You ain't going to be you. Not you. You're
not going to be you. That's it. See, it's my responsibility to
prepare you for the last moment, because everybody here
is going to be headed for the last moment. You wouldn't
be here at this lecture otherwise. Everybody's headed for
the last moment, and unless you hear the truth, you won't
know what to do. Therefore, karmically I am laying down
that I have spoken the truth. That last moment you will
get, "Walk straight ahead, no matter what. Die for God."
And as you lay down your life, the agony of death arises,
and it is agonizing and you do die. And then before you
stands the splendor, that what you thought was life was
not life anyway.

But because it is so real, you see why you've guarded it
all these lifetimes. It's convincingly real that it is your life,
that it is the source of your life.

* * *

The ego is very, very strong, or it wouldn't have survived all these lifetimes. At this last moment, it tells you
or you feel that it's the very source of your life that you're

laying down, and at that point I'm telling you it is safe to surrender. It is safe, but you have to have a knowingness that it's safe. You have to have heard it. You have to know it. You have to have it in your aura. And then suddenly out of nowhere, it comes to you. Walk right through. The Zen saying to walk into fear, no matter what got me through it. "No matter what" means without limitation, even to death itself. No matter what, and so I repeat the words of the master who I followed at that moment: no matter what.

All right, so as you surrender, as you're willing to let go, you'll see the ego hangs on because it's getting something out of it. Now, everybody's ego is going to resist this. Expect it to. Let's hear it from the old ego. Oh, this hatred is justified. I should feel angry at this guy—you know what I mean. It's very clever at convincing you that the juice it's getting is justified, good for America, if nothing else, and they deserve it anyway. To give up self-pity, to give up anger, to give up resentment, to surrender them through forgiveness—so the power, of course, in the *Course in Miracles* is the willingness to forgive all and get out of the lower fields of consciousness. So in the beginning the ego kind of identifies with form. That's here. How does it know that? Because it registers it through recognition. You'll notice that there isn't any *me* that's thinking anyway. There is a watcher, experiencer.

In meditation or in contemplation, if you focus on the field, you'll notice that witnessing is happening of its own. There's no *me* deciding to be aware of all the people in this room. It's happening automatically. For every one of you, it's happening automatically, your awareness of everybody here. Isn't that so? It's not because you're saying, "Oh, I choose to be aware of everybody in the room." It's happening by itself. There's no point in taking credit for it.

You don't get credit for being aware of everything that's going on in the room, because it's happening of its own.

So the first thing you notice about consciousness is it's automatic. The light of consciousness is automatic. It expresses as the watcher, the experiencer through awareness, the observer. You get to the source of that faculty, you'll see that's an impersonal faculty. There isn't any personal *you* that decided to be consciously aware. Witnessing is happening of its own. So in meditation, you pull back from identifying with the content of meditation—I am this, I did that, and all that b.s.; that's all fallacious story—and you realize that that which I am is the witness of all those thoughts, feelings, and that panorama. I call it a phantasmagoria. It's such a wonderful word. I love that word, *phantasmagoria*. My great-aunt used to have something for us that was really special for your birthday, stuff she called a monster Polyfeme. And she puts that under there; she said, "That's a monster Polyfeme." That would be something like a whole croquet set or something, you know. Monster Polyfeme.

So this whole phantasmagoria goes through the mind, you know. Everybody that's meditated knows that—memories, thoughts, fantasies, imaginations, little itty-bitty-boop-ba-bid-de-bop-bop music from the 1920s that you heard from all this garbage. So you realize that that which you are is the involuntary witness. You don't volunteer to be the witness. You are the witness. No point in taking credit for it. No point to feel ashamed about it because it's automatic. Consciousness automatically is conscious because that's its nature, and it's impersonal. That's part of your karmic inheritance, is to be conscious. So one begins to identify with the witness, the observer, then with consciousness, then one stops identifying the consciousness as personal, and one even goes beyond the manifest and realizes the ultimate is beyond all form, the unmanifest, out of which consciousness arises. And that makes you a Buddha.

Karma is a very simple thing. It's argued in Christianity and all, but that's all superfluous. Whether Jesus taught about it or not, it's all irrelevant. You know, if it's a reality, it's a reality whether Jesus taught about it or not. What did he know 2,000 years ago, you know what I mean? We don't know what he said. It was in a different language, a different culture, on the other side of the world thousands of years ago, so how do you know what he said? That's why we find calibrating levels of consciousness very, very useful, because you can say, "Did he really say that?" and you can test it.

So people that are dedicated to spiritual truth, then, will find that the reason I like certain nondenominational kinds of endeavors, such as this congregation and others like it, is not because it is committed to some historical event thousands of years ago, to some other culture in some other land, some other continent, in some other language that hasn't been spoken for 1,000 years, and now you're supposed to take it verbatim—but it's more the spiritual reality that you can verify in the here and now. Every enlightened mystic throughout all of time has said exactly the same thing. There's been no variation at all. And I like spiritual enterprises that are dedicated to the basic spiritual principles and truth, which prevails in all religion and which is intrinsic to the teaching of any mystic.

Anybody who's realized the truth will say exactly the same thing, because it's not possible to say anything else. Why? Because there's no personal self to twist the truth. It has no investment in doing so—has no gain, no loss.

Consequently, the undistorted truth is always the same. Krishna couldn't have said anything different than what was said today. He couldn't say anything different than what Christ said. Couldn't say anything different than what Buddha said or any other mystic. There's only one truth, and it's only knowable subjectively; the source of one's own existence, the radical subjective presence of the self as God imminent is the only absolute knowable possible. There is no other knowable possible. There is talking about, but the only way one can know is to be it. You can know about a cat, but unless you are a cat friend, you're talking through your head. Only a cat knows what cat-ness is. That's a fact. We've confirmed that many times. The authority on cat-ness in our family is the cat.

I was once the chief of staff of a recovery home for teenage girls. One of the girls told me she wanted to get out of this place. She was in the best place she's ever been in her life, but she wanted out. She's lived with cruelty, poverty, the slums, drugs, and sexual abuse, physical abuse, so then she goes out in the street, gets stoned, steals something, gets put in jail. Now she's put in the best residential treatment program in the country—private schools, exclusive academy, equestrian services, 35 beautiful horses, 150 acres of individual counseling, a great psychiatrist. World's best of everything. But she still wants out of here.

This is the graspingness—the ego's self is greedy. And so she says, "I want freedom," and the way she gets it is by being violently bad. In fact, the more you won't let her out, the more violent she gets. She punches holes in the wall. She threatens to kill herself. She cuts on herself, threatens suicide, homicide, and everything. So here she is, in the cage of her own creation, and this is the way she thinks she's going to get the bananas. So after some counseling with her, I said, "You know how you get the bananas?" She said no. I said, "You've got to turn your back on the bananas because this is the different way to freedom."

So if we want enlightenment, we've got a solar plexus desire, a compulsive, obsessive drivenness about it. We think it's a getting-ness. No.

* * *

What do you think was behind all those wars? Testosterone. I mean, all the damage, crime, murder, mayhem, and all, that's all testosterone gone crazy in the world. It is. All that testosterone out there, it killed 10 million people in the last century. For the führer, dedicate your testosterone to the führer. That's what it's all about, isn't it? Prove you're a man. Prove you're brave. Be aggressive. Get out there and be a good killer.

So to reach enlightenment, then, we have to turn our back on that, because what's necessary, then, is to surrender everything to God. And the arms come through the bars here. First it's a banana. Then it's a million dollars. And as we let go of that, suddenly we realize that all the time we were free. We were free all this time, searching for freedom, and we already are. Let go of worrying about survival because the field of the self automatically guarantees your survival until your karmically destined end. The ego says, "If it wasn't for me, you wouldn't make it. If it wasn't for me, you wouldn't remember to take your vitamins." No. The reason you remember to take your vitamins is because your ego is prompted by your Self. The infinite field that knows that you're destined to hang out here till 97 years old *also* knows that you'll need vitamins to do it, and it prompts the ego to say, "Hey, I better check my cholesterol." Then you do the *Course in Miracles* and you think cholesterol can't kill you—that it's all in your head. You can go back to eating cheeseburgers. You can leave here when you leave here. You know what I mean?

Serious spiritual work, then, tends to sort of exhilarate. It's sort of a karmic field behind it. There's times when it's interesting. Then you leave it alone. Then you come across a new book and you get going in it again. You think it's coming from out there. It's not coming from out there. It's coming from the cyclic karmic propensities within you. And something really grabs you, and you start to really get moving on it, and the momentum sort of builds up. And then there comes a point where it becomes the primary focus of your being, and at that point the great drive to reach the end starts. You're willing to walk away from everything, throw it in the back of your truck and drive away from it all.

So we all know that the way to God is well traveled, that we're not alone, because we're all together as one in doing so. Everybody on the planet right now is going to be off the planet. We all come on the planet at the same time. All of us in the room are going to be on the other side before long, right? Come on and off. So we come on, I think to a degree, by the level of inspiration of a group. That's sort of what pulls you together, a shared inspiration. It's not conscious. It's not really spoken, but there's a knowingness to it, you know, that we belong to each other and with each other.

At times in our lives, each of us feels alone. It is difficult during such times to grasp the idea that we are all one. We are part of the divine and never alone. It can be helpful to meditate or contemplate on this, exploring how you are actually one with all of existence. Perhaps you can practice using all of your senses as you do this exploration. Go out into nature, explore, feel, and smell into the trees and flowers. As you eat, taste into the food, knowing that it, too, is part of you and part of the divinity that is all. As you observe others throughout your day, you may take some time to explore the connections you have to each and every individual that you meet. You may wish to connect with your celestial angels and guides, again feeling into the oneness that you have with them. Give yourself permission to fully experience the oneness with all of existence and open your heart and mind to your connection with all.

CHAPTER 11

Relief from Human Suffering

Where is your heart calling you? If you're not sure, perhaps you'd like to reflect on your life, noting what most moves you, what most inspires you. Going back to your early childhood and into the present day and marking any areas of life you are most drawn to can prove to be helpful. Part of the courage to step boldly rests in putting out our spiritual intentions, then surrendering them to the divine, having faith that all will occur just as it should.

In this chapter, Dr. Hawkins expands on the power of surrendering, both to the silence and to our desires. He ends this session providing you with a pearl, the most powerful and accessible tool at your disposal as you continue on your journey of enlightenment.

You can't see "out there" until you've already seen it within yourself. The willingness to surrender positionality out of humility to God means that one is then ready to accept the possibility that intrinsically men are innocent and that they're suffering from a profound ignorance, and that the only way out of suffering, then, is to transcend that ignorance for spiritual truth. So then, one becomes a student of spiritual truth in their personal life or even eventually in their professional life, you see. The relief of human suffering, then, is what medicine is about, what psychiatry is about. It's why I went into psychoanalysis. Each of those things was to sharpen the capacity to assist in the relief of human suffering in all of its forms, whether it's psychopharmacology or understanding unconscious conflicts. If you're dedicated to that endeavor, one eventually ends up with spiritual truth and spiritual programs, because to many human dilemmas there is no other answer, just like there's no other answer to the death of a loved one except to surrender to God and the will of God and the knowingness that eventually spiritual truth will heal all pain.

The way we transcend all of that, again, goes back to humility and the willingness to let go of the way we see things and allow a spiritual truth, which comes in of its own. People don't realize that when one becomes silent, out of that silence all of a sudden arises a realization. We try to force an answer or force God to give us an answer with a demand. Many prayers are nothing but demands. We try to force God to respond to our demand, which is disguised as a prayer. You are trying to force God to give you a new Ford. When we actually surrender to God's will, suddenly we see it differently, and when we see it differently, we realize there is no loss. The source of the pain disappears, and when the source of the pain disappears, the source came out of ignorance and came out of the way we're seeing it. By constant surrender to God, all things resolve themselves, even very advanced and complicated spiritually very difficult issues.

The best way to handle a prayer for a Ford is to surrender your desire for a Ford. Why did you want the Ford? Because you think that happiness is something outside of yourself. If I have the new Ford, then I will feel successful and then I will feel happy. So all desires, then, have associated with them the unconscious belief system that they will bring us happiness, but that makes us very dependent on the external world. And so our happiness is always vulnerable, and therefore, we live in fear all the time, because if the source of happiness is outside yourself, you're always in a weak and possibly victim position. If the source of happiness, then, is self-fulfillment within one's self, then nobody can take it away from you, and even to reach a point whether you physically live or die is really irrelevant. Many times you're, like, looking death in the face, and if you leave, you leave and if you don't, you don't. And it's no big deal, frankly.

When we get beset by a desire, then, we've set ourselves up for suffering, and therefore, if we're willing to surrender everything to God, see, devotional nonduality means out of devotion to truth and to God we're willing to surrender everything and anything no matter what, even life itself. Then it's resolved, and something replaces it that is better than the new Ford would have been.

I think the most practical of all the spiritual techniques, frankly, is contemplation. Why is that? Because there's two different styles of contemplation, and there's two comparative styles of meditation. There's one I call central focus and the other I call peripheral focus. In meditation, then, one can be intensely focused on what one imagines to be the moment and to constantly let go wanting to change it and surrender to God as it arises, and this is concentrating on the focus of the field. In contemplation, one does the same thing. One focuses intently on the task that is at hand, peeling a potato, whatever one is doing. One focuses fixedly on the focus of attention at the moment and lets go wanting to change it. In other words, it's constantly surrendering to the moment as the moment arises.

In the more peripheral style of meditation and contemplation, instead of focusing on the focus, one focuses on the field. I think that is the faster technique in which one is always aware of the field instead of the focus. So people that are focused on the field then walk into a room, and they instantly pick up the energy of the room, the general gist of what's happening in the room. And if you ask them what anybody in the room looked like, they wouldn't be able to tell you because they didn't focus on that. They were picking up on what is the ambiance, the overall energy, what is the state of the prevailing condition? For instance, one can quickly pick that up and then try to define it later. But if you go into contemplation or meditation on the field itself, because the field is closer to the ultimate reality, I think it's faster and more effective. You see, because the reason you're focused on some specific is because of intention. As you shift your focus to the field, then, you're transcending intention, and it's more of a surrendering to prevalent conditions rather than trying to change them. The same occurs, then, in closed-eye meditation, where you sit quietly and you watch the content of the mind without any intention of changing it. You watch the thoughts drift by—the images, the memories, the fantasies, the imaginations—and instead of focusing on the content of thinkingness, one begins to focus on what is the field in which this thinkingness is occurring. If we do that, we notice, as I mentioned before, that primarily 99 percent of the mind is actually quite silent, is merely watching and witnessing, and so you begin to transcend identification with the content of thought and begin to move into the watcher, the witness of the thinkingness.

So instead of thinking, "I am the mind," one then moves in and becomes witness of the mind, watcher of the mind, and eventually it comes to you that you are the field in which the witness and the watcher is cognizant of the content of the consciousness. And then it suddenly comes upon one's self that one is the infinite field out of which consciousness itself arises, before time and all the concepts of time, before perception, before any belief in something such as causation. So the mind stops thinking, trying to figure it out. It stops memorizing. It stops editing. It stops its self-justification. And you'll notice that the mind, in its ordinary state, spends a great deal of time on speculation, rehashing, trying to reinterpret the past, trying to find a better way of looking at one's self and past events, self-excuses, blaming others. And so this mind, then, is sort of an endless phantasmagoria.

And instead of being the victim of the mind, and say, "How can I make my mind stop thinking?" Or "I go to bed at night and my mind just keeps on thinking." One can transcend the identification with the content of mind, and it doesn't take much effort. In fact, it's quite easy to really allow yourself to surrender and realize that one is the witness of the thinking, one is the field of awareness of the thinking, and identify with consciousness itself, with the realization that the higher truth is that one is consciousness itself and not the content of consciousness. Next comes the realization of what is the source of consciousness, and with the realization of the source of consciousness, one then enters into a field of knowingness in which the knower and the known are one and the same thing. And at that point, one has transcended duality, and one sees there is no difference between the knower and the known, that they are one and the same. And one realizes and becomes identified with the source of existence itself, the source of consciousness itself, and with that, there arises a feeling of being at home.

So the feeling of coming into that field of awareness, then, is like one has spent their whole lifetime being homesick and finally is at home again. That sense of self is more central than the pronoun sense of self. What one thought one was one's self is really quite peripheral to the reality of that which is the true Self. And so you move from the self with the small *s* to the Self with a large *s*, and then one is home at last. The easiest move is from the content of thinkingness to the witness of thinkingness. It doesn't take any great genius. Somebody complains that their thinking is driving them crazy, and I say, "Well, how do you know that?" Well, because I experience it. Well, so then, you're not the thoughts. You're the experiencer of the thoughts, or you wouldn't be complaining. The thoughts are not complaining. The thoughts are not saying, "Help, help, help." No, it's the experiencer of the thoughts. So you see, I am the experiencer of the thoughts.

Now, how do you know what thoughts you're experiencing? Because you're witnessing them. You're registering them. So you can move out of identification with the content of consciousness, the thinkingness, to be the watcher, the witness, the experiencer, and that already takes you one step out of it. So you're no longer the victim of it. You're the witness of it. You're not in the accident. You're a bystander. So you move from being in the accident to being the bystander of the accident. You're the witness of the tragedy. You're the witness of the thinkingness. You're the witness of the self-blame. So with a little meditation and a little contemplation it's easy to realize that that which you really are is the experiencer witness. You're the experiencer witness. You're not what is being witnessed. You're not the picture on the wall, obviously. And you can't be the memory because what you're thinking about was yesterday and today is today, unless you can also be in yesterday and today at the same time. Obviously that which you are is the witness of the thoughts. What we complain about is the experience.

So then we move to feelings. So we are not our thoughts. We're not the mind. The next move is to move out of the feelings. We talked before about feelings, how feelings are a way of feeding on one's self. The ego feeds on indignation. It feeds on self-pity. So you watch the mind, and you see that I'm not the content of the thoughts. Well, what about the feelings that go with them? You look at the feelings and you'll see that these feelings are feeding off themselves. If you're strictly honest with yourself, you realize that you're getting a lot out of being the victim. You're getting a lot out of being the wronged one. You're getting a lot out of being the misunderstood one. Now you have to be willing to surrender the payoff. You have to be willing to surrender the juice you get out of being the victim, the wronged one, the misunderstood one, the neglected one, the abused one, and when you let go of what you're getting out of victimhood and pain and suffering and righteousness and all these payoffs.

So the way to escape from the feelingness is the payoff that one gets out of them. Am I willing to surrender the payoff I'm getting out of this, and is my love and devotion to God greater than my self-victimization? So you begin to see that you're not the victim of anything out there, that all victimization is a self-victimization. Even if you are in the viewpoint of the world, let's say, the victim of an accident. Well, the pain and suffering you get out of the accident is sort of a byproduct of the ego. Let's say, you lose a finger in an accident. Well, one can immerse one's self in anger, rage, indignation, self-pity, or one can just totally surrender it to God and say, "I don't know what it means or why it happened." And it may be some time before you get the realization of the karmic setup for that to happen.

But as you see it, once you get what it is, then it's an all right. It's an okayness. So suffering, a great deal of suffering, comes out of, it's really the consequence of spiritual ignorance. As we said, all the great avatars have said that the basic problem with being human is really profound ignorance. So spiritual research and consciousness research is designed to overcome that ignorance about ourselves, about the human condition, about the nature of consciousness itself, about spiritual reality, and then utilize that knowledge to free ourselves from the fetters that have bound us through all these lifetimes, or we would have all become Buddhas already.

✳ ✳ ✳

So a lot of people say, you know, "I don't have time to meditate." And that's why I favor contemplation, because contemplation continues all the time, everywhere. It eventually becomes a habit, a way of being in the world, in which you really don't cling to anything. If the movie starts, it starts, and if it doesn't, you do something else. So this not being at the effect of the world, not being at the effect of the mind, if you become more and more merged and identified with the field in which all the phenomena are occurring, then you become more and more independent of the content of life. You can sit in the field and meditate or you can sit in the movie and ignore the movie and meditate. So you can have the TV on and completely ignore it. So one's inner state, then, is independent, and it's a matter of choice. You can either watch the movie or not watch the movie. One can either become involved in it or detach from it. But that's volitional, and for the average person that's not volitional. They have to change the channel because they're at the effect of the channel.

So to transcend the identification with the content of consciousness is the fastest way to a state in which you let everything go as it arises. So this takes us back to intentionality. The intention, then, of devotion to God means the willingness to surrender willfulness to God. At all times we're always surrendering willfulness. As we said, the juice we get out of the ego is coming out of the willfulness to juice the ego. When you let go of that willfulness to pull all the juice you can out of it, then it stops, when you don't get any satisfaction out of it. We surrender the will. So the fastest way to God, of course, and the one, let's say, Ramana Maharshi and spiritual teachers such as that said you can either follow a lifetime of spiritual techniques and meditation and things like that, or you can surrender to God at great depth. So to surrender to God at great depth can take a split second, but to arrive at that second can take lifetimes of agony and suffering. However, spiritual information then shortens the period of time that it takes to get there. To wait for that moment to arrive spontaneously may take, as the Buddha said, eons of time. With spiritual preparation, then, to have heard certain spiritual truth shortens that time dramatically. Now at least one is aware of what the problem is.

The persistence in willfulness, then, is what precludes enlightenment, that and that alone, one single thing, the insistence on what I want, what I desire, how I see it—so the personal *I* and its imperatives are always standing in the way. The willingness to surrender one's willfulness to God, devotional nonduality, means the love of God is so intense that one is willing to surrender one's personal will. One comes face to face with it at the final moment, let's say, through all these lifetimes and through spiritual techniques and evolution. One begins to transcend the ego and begins to loosen its hold. The listening of trying to dominate things with one's will and change them lessens, and surrender comes up now as a style and a way of being.

So as everything arises, it's surrendered to God to be what it is at the moment, without any desire to change it. The surrender of one's willfulness then pulls the props up from the ego, which weakens and collapses, and one goes into an incredible state. In that incredible state of an infinite knowingness, there is no person present that does the knowing. It's knowingness knowing itself, and then comes the only possible moment of death. All the previous times, one left the body—very often it was a joke. Very often it was great relief. A lot of times it was actually comical, aside from all the drama that people put onto it. The actual experience itself is, frankly, quite a relief a lot of times, and one's glad to be rid of it and out of there.

So one never does experience death, and all the lifetimes of feared death all end up to be a joke, you know. But there is one death and one death only that one can experience, and now that death begins to arise as a profound-seeming reality, because that which one feels, knows, senses, has always been the core of one's sense of self, the core of one's own existence, now comes up and stands between one and the ultimate reality. And one gets now that one is being asked to surrender one's actual life to God, what you believe to be your life, which you've always experienced as the core and the essence, the very center, the very source of life itself. One is confronted with this surrender of one's life to God. In that instant, then, there comes the knowingness from some higher spiritual reality, which does not speak verbally, but it's a knowingness that comes to you because you've heard it from those who have become enlightened in their lifetime. Surrender all to God, no matter what—no matter what, including fear of loss of life, including what you believe to be your life itself. If you have a decision over what you consider to be the source of life itself, then you do not have within you a handle on the source of life itself, because that which is the source of life itself is not something you can surrender.

So you're faced with surrendering what you think is the very core and essence of your own existence. The fact that you think that already indicates that it's fallacious. Some intuitive greater knowingness that comes from the great beings who have been through that path comes to you, and then the great faith—that's why it's called devotional—comes up, and you find that within you, you actually have the capacity to surrender your life itself to the unknown. The known all that you believed through all these lifetimes is the core and source of your own life, and you must now surrender this to God. And in that final moment, one does die, and there is a split second of agony as one feels one's self, at least in this particular instance. There is the actual agony of dying, the first and only time you've ever experienced it. After a brief second of what seems like unbearable agony, one feels one's self dying and suddenly explodes in realization that no death is possible, that you are the source of all that has ever existed, throughout all of time, before all universes, after all universes, that which you are is untouchable. And the source of existence itself is not different than the truth and reality of that which you are. And from that point on, death is impossible because there's no one to die. There's no one left to die because there is no one now. Having surrendered the one you thought was the self, yourself, the oneness of yourself, because it's gone, there's nothing left to die. And so the fear of death is extinguished forever.

And then at that point, everything is happening spontaneously, and one is the witness of it, and it takes considerable time, at least in this particular instance, to learn how to navigate within the world itself because the body walks about by itself, everything is happening spontaneously. The best one can do is try to reenergize the mind to at least second-guess it and appear as normal, relating to what the world considers "normal," in order to stay in the world. In this case, that was not possible, and it was necessary to leave the world for some years, and even now very often how the body navigates is absolutely a mystery. The universe does it somehow. You see the body moves about by itself spontaneously, so something obviously is moving it, but there isn't any source or central spot of volition that through intention designs how it will move or what it will do. It just goes about itself automatically.

And that's what's called, I guess, in Jungian terms the *persona*, that which interfaces with the world and reflects back the world. So what the world sees is that which the world is reflecting back upon itself, but there is no central reality to it, because one is the field, not the content of the field. And what is witnessed is the content of the field. It's not what one does anymore. It's what one is to the world, and how one holds consciousness of mankind. The service now moves from the individual to the field itself, just as one's identification with the field is discontinued.

Then one's identification with the field energizes the field. And so one tries to serve the evolution of consciousness of mankind as it stands at this moment and to serve God in whatever one's capacity is occurring. However, it's occurring of its own, so one neither takes credit nor discredit.

* * *

Frequently you have permission to leave the body. Actually, the permission is a standing permission at any moment. The permission becomes more obvious at times. There's times in the middle of a lecture when it gets very strong that it's hard to explain in ordinary terms. It's a knowingness that one is invited to leave at this moment, not only permitted but almost invited, attracted to leave. There's no way of knowing what decision will be made because there's nobody making the decisions, so one watches. If the body falls over and stops breathing, well, then it went that way. And if it keeps on walking down the aisle, then it went that way. But one doesn't know until one sees what happens.

The closest came one time during the middle of a lecture, when I walked down the aisle—or my body walked down, what the world calls *I*—and there was a strong pull to leave, as though one is being pulled back into heaven, you know, like by a magnet or something. And so one didn't know if it was going to keep on walking or not keep on walking. And it, by some mystical means, it kept on walking and so it still is. There are many things that really cannot be explained in terms that are comprehensible by ordinary thinkingness, you know. People are able to comprehend it, you might say unconsciously, or by via the field of their own spiritual reality, so the spiritual reality is able to comprehend what was just said, but the mind and the ego really can't because there's no terminology that is correct in the world of verbalization that really adequately describes it.

But I think people have been in dream states and all that, and people in near-death experiences know that very well. You can either leave or not leave. You know, when I was a teenager and had that experience in the snowbank, it was quite similar, because breathing stopped; everything came to an absolute still perfection. One didn't have to keep breathing or resume the physical body at all, but at that instant, I saw it in my father. If the body had not resumed breathing, my father would have presumed I was dead, because he believed in death, you know. I mean, everybody believes in death. Well, at a certain state, you realize death is not possible, but I saw that he didn't know that, so he would be grieving what he thought was death, you know, so I breathed again. See, death is not a possibility. The energy of life can be transformed from one form to another, but it cannot be extinguished, just like the law of the conservation of energy or the law of the conservation of matter. The law of the conservation of life is that life cannot be extinguished.

Dr. Hawkins ends this chapter reminding us that we are not our physical bodies and that our spirit, our true essence, does not die. Given this truth, how much do you apply it to your current fears around your death and the death of your loved ones? You might like to try a visualization in which you imagine your death but experience the continued life of your essence thereafter.

CHAPTER 12

Removing the Obstacles to Love

* ✳ *

Going into this chapter, you might ask yourself how your family, your job, your country, and the world as a whole might transform as you begin to. Giving yourself permission to enter the realm of the possible, how might your world change?

As you progress through this chapter, you may wish to reflect on how you can start to apply the wisdom and insights you've gained from this book into your spiritual life.

When we talk about surrender to the truth, commitment to the truth, then, the pathway of nonduality is you're committed to the truth for its own sake because truth is an expression of divinity. Truth is divinity expressed in a form comprehensible by man, because truth stands present as the source of one's existence at all times, but it's not knowable by man because he pays no attention to it. All right. So the truth, then, has to be what you're devoted to, so the chips fall wherever they fall. Now, that willingness to surrender any vested interest in the answer is where people have difficulty. They want you to calibrate their favorite guru and tell you that he's the savior of mankind. I get favorite gurus for the avatars that are saving mankind every week by the dozen, and they always calibrate about 289 or something.

They're sweet, adorable people, so we make them what we want them to be. We project that onto them. On a certain level we're seeing truth because it is true that love itself is the salvation of mankind. So very often the worshiper is of a higher consciousness than the supposed avatar, and what's happening is they're projecting their unconditional lovingness and thinking that Mother Blah-Blah-Something is going to save mankind. It's their heart they're projecting onto that person and seeing them as the great savior. So their naiveté is touching, you know, when they ask me, "What does she calibrate at?" I don't really know how to answer because I know they think that she's going to be 800, and I know it's 284.

So our dedication to truth then has to be that I want to know the truth because I want to know the truth, and then you get honest answers, to have no vested interest. Now, the technique itself, as I told you, the energy is quick, so we don't want any background music playing. Music that calibrates at 700 would throw everything off. You want peace and quiet, and you don't want to have distractions.

Now, this is not a time for affection either. She's a patient; I'm the doctor. We're clinical with each other. It's detached. We're just asking an objective fact, like we want to know the voltage on this battery. Then I press down with only a couple ounces of pressure. I'm pushing down. I'm not trying to break her arm. See, certain parts of the world we've been, they were all like into mesomorphism, you know, like they're all muscle and pushing down and the guy's like, "This is not a test of strength, folks." This is you're trying to get how much resistance is there to about that much pressure.

So as I pressed down, she resists to the same degree I am pressing down. The person I'm holding in mind is over 200. Resist. Now, sometimes you'll get different answers than what you expected. That's something different.

When you're calibrating numbers or you're calibrating yes and no—the simplest thing is simple yes and no. As I said, we found out it's not yes or no. It's yes or not yes. And today we didn't get into quantum mechanics, but there's the mathematics of advanced theoretical physics, and eventually quantum mechanics takes you into the fact that nature can only say yes; it cannot say no. It says yes or not yes, and this is concordant with quantum mechanics, the Heisenberg principle as interpreted by process one and process two. You find the only answer you can get is either a yes or a not yes. You cannot get a no out of the universe. The universe doesn't know no.

When you ask the question the second time, you think you're asking the same question. You're not, because when you've asked the question, according to the Heisenberg principle of quantum mechanics, you've already changed the reality. It's not the same reality. The fact that you've already asked it has already changed the potentiality. In fact, the more yeses you get, the more yes becomes fixated. It's called, it has a name, "exhilarated guessing things" tend to make them consistently yes. I knew you were dying of curiosity about quantum mechanics, so I thought I'd bring that up. The application of the Heisenberg principle is that once you've asked the question, you've already changed the potentiality. Why? Because you've discharged the potentiality, you've closed the—you've collapsed the wave. Yes, because of the Dirac equation you've collapsed the wave, you know, and now you're stuck with what is a new reality now, observation again.

We recently did some research for somebody, and at the beginning it sounded sort of simple. You know, would this be good for that or would this be good for that? And we started getting ambiguous answers. Then we got that, uh-oh, this is far more complicated than just asking numbers or yes or no, because when you say, you know, this is good for this, you've got to define what you mean by *good*. Good person, good potential. Then we got into, "Is this person karmically equipped to handle this thing at this point? Are they karmically destined to be able to handle that?" Then we were asking questions about something that is in a process, so then we had to say, "Is this person good at this time or would they be concordant with the direction in which this process is going?" You see what I'm saying? Is this a good coach for this team? Well, but this team is just adding two new strong members from a whole different coaching background, and, in view of that, this coach, is he still going to be the best coach? Well, he may not be because these two guys coming in from a different coaching background are not going to jibe with this coach. So you see how complex it is.

All right. So instead of a simple yes or no, very often what you get into is a whole research session—and I'm thinking of the one that we just did yesterday—would really take a good part of a day, a good part of an afternoon, which was seriously tracked down because you're dealing with algorithms in a way, algorithms and variables and potentialities, so under what conditions, you see. As we said on the whiteboard, the truth cannot be defined unless you define the context, to the truth of yes or no would be then under what conditions. That's why I like situational ethics, because what is ethical in one situation is not ethical in another, and I know there are religious disciplines that pooh-pooh situational ethics. They have the right to be wrong.

* * *

How do we cultivate more love or get more love in our life? We can't. What you do is remove the obstacles to love, because love is the essence of that which you are. We saw this morning, war is not the opposite of peace. Peace is the natural condition when falsehood is removed. So lovingness is the automatic condition when the obstructions to it, which are false and fallacious, are removed. So lovingness becomes a way of being; love is not an emotion. It goes from here to there. You can't lose love. Somebody can't run off with love.

* * *

Can science ever evolve beyond the 499 level? No. Quantum mechanics was a hope. Quantum mechanics calibrates about 466, 465. If you could get there with science, Einstein calibrated at 499. You see, after the Copenhagen conference in 1927, where quantum mechanics was discussed, and all the greats—Bohr and Born and Heisenberg and Dirac—were all there, all the great names in advanced theoretical physics, Einstein had his response to the Heisenberg principle, that says when your consciousness focuses on something, you've already changed it. You've collapsed the wave function of the potential energy field. Einstein said he didn't want consciousness to come into what he hoped would be an independent, objective, definable, provable, external objective universe independent of human consciousness.

And therefore, he set them down, 499. Cut himself off. Born on the other hand, who calibrates over 500, talked about the universe, the enfolded and the unfolded. So he calibrates over 500, and Freud also. Freud was correct when he said the gods of old—the vicious, angry god who's going to get even with you for sin and has his favorites and all—he says this is all coming out of the unconscious, the child's fear of the great big parent out there. And so what Freud said was correct. The false gods are false, but then he made the illogical jump that the false gods are false; therefore there isn't a true. He didn't prove there wasn't a true one. He just proved that the false gods were false, which already was an advance because it took him to 499, which is—499 is pretty good. Einstein and Newton and Freud, at 499, that's pretty advanced, but it is not the realm of 500, because at 500 you have to move to the subjective. Where we all live is in the subjective.

We use objective terminology, but we all live in the here and the now of the subjective. It's the undefinable, subtle quality of all experience. That's what we're experiencing all the time in the out-there-ness of what we think is causing it is really irrelevant. Where we live is from moment to moment, is in the subjective. All of your life is lived in the subjective. You never live it in the objective, because even if you look at the objective, you're only doing it from the experiential quality of the subjective. So only a verifiable objective reality is real, that's a very subjective statement. He's already concluding that his subjective truth about that is what's true. That's a very subjective and very egoistic kind of a view of it, that only your view of it is what is.

* * *

What is the astral level? There's other dimensions. There's the spiritual and the astral, and the spiritually naïve confuse the two. The New Age festival is the carnival of the astral. Every kind of psychic reading, ba-ba-hoo-hoo on the other side, and cast the runes, cast the stones, cast the necklaces, cast your toenails. I mean, you know what I mean. The astrological signs coming from Master Baba on the other side tell you that you should buy resources right now and sell your ranch to your mother-in-law. That would be $1,500. You don't want to get caught in the circus. It's intriguing. Never underestimate it. There are many energies in this universe that would not like to see you advance spiritually. Very definitely.

And they are very adept at it. Extremely clever. They're more clever than you are. They've been at it for a long time. The art of spiritual seduction and glamour is why many gurus who wrote books that calibrated in the 500s, now you calibrate them and they're 180. Hm. The glamour and seduction, power over others. So the downside of the spiritual teacher, then, is power over others, appearing special, claiming unique connections and powers and telling somebody, "Well, you're the third incarnation of the fifth whatchamacalit lama who was the descendant of the Baba hierarchy." Boy, you feel good about that. And you're now nowhere, folks, because you've just been had.

No, it's hard to define the astral, which is higher, middle, and lower. Higher is celestial; middle astral is where all kinds of good people go in between lifetimes, and lower astral is where bin Laden and all those people get their energy from, their inspiration, Adolph Hitler and all, drives those. Lower astral, then, is the demonic, you might say. The middle astral is the so-called inner planes, and the higher astral is celestial. So many people get communications via the celestial, and you're talking with angels and things. So when you calibrate what is the source of the information on the other side it will tell you whether it's higher, middle, or lower. Ouija boards and things like that you will find calibrate extremely low. You think they're just a game. They're not a game, *Dungeons and Dragons*. Many of the computer games that right now think it's so much fun to track down and kill women, etc., you know, they calibrate around 80. You're going to sit there and program your mind with an energy field of 80? And what you do is you set up programming, and then one moment your mind goes blank, and "I don't know why I kill them. They just—I just wanted to see what it's like to kill people. Just wanted to see what it's like to kill people."

There's another thing you're not aware of and that is that when you think your conscious mind is conscious, it's unconscious about 24 percent of the time. That's why I tell people to buy radar detectors. God says to buy radar detectors. When you think you're being conscious, you're actually unconscious over 20 percent of the time, 22 percent, 23 percent, 24 percent, 25 percent. Roughly 23 to 24 percent of the time, you're unconscious and thinking that you're conscious. This is self-hypnosis. You think you're conscious. Twenty-three percent of the time, you are not conscious. And you think you are. That's the bad side, is that when you're unconscious you don't think you are. You think you're being conscious. Twenty-three percent of the time you're unconscious. If you don't think so, get a radar detector, and you'll quickly see how true it is. There's no cop there. There's nobody down the street. All of a sudden, it goes off. Well, where did he come from? He was there all along, folks. You were just asleep.

Quantum mechanics tells you that once you get past the macroscopic world to the microscopic, you're dealing with improbability, and what the ego deals with is probability. Skydivers, good luck, because you can do it 18 times in a row and the 19th time, just as you go, you get a thought of your dead mother-in-law and you forgot to send her flowers, and that was the second. It cost you your life, see. So extreme sports, you're forgetting that 24 percent of the time you're unconscious, so nine times off the springboard doing five gainers on the way down; the next time a broken neck. So you can't count on that which is unreliable to be constantly reliable.

There were friends of mine in Sedona who owned an animal place. These guys were well known in town, and when you had a rattlesnake, you called them up. They were private guys, and they would come over and pick up the rattlesnake for you. And lots of people don't want rattlesnakes in their yard, so it was free, and they got to keep the rattlesnake.

So this pair, one of them got bit 19 times by a rattlesnake, 19 times, 19 bites, and survived 19 times. And the 20th rattlesnake bite killed him. The 20th. Well, you see how easily we're fooled: 19 times; I'm immune. No, you're not immune, because the 20th time, you were unconscious. So, therefore, I say the purpose of a radar detector is humility, to remind you that you cannot depend on the ego for your own survival. Your survival is dependent on the field, and the field is telling you to get a radar detector. It's to remind you that 24 percent of the time you're unconscious.

✳ ✳ ✳

If death is set at the time of birth, are events in your life preordained? No. You see, karma means that your soul has evolved over a period of time, and now you're coming in at a certain level and certain choices are available at that level. This choice is not available there, and this choice is not available there, so our level of consciousness to some degree determines our choices. I just didn't get the choice to be a fullback. And head of the swimming team says, "Shorty, you don't have a long enough stroke." Football coach says, "We don't want you on the field." So I went for boxing. They told me they don't have anything that small—they went from flyweight to mosquito weight—anybody who's under 90 pounds. So you see, I didn't have the choice to be a heavyweight champion. So karmically you're already destined.

We hope you've enjoyed this book. We encourage you to refer back to it repeatedly and often. Following this fascinating journey, you'll see how easy it is to raise your consciousness to the levels of power rather than force, so that you, too, can become one of those who is awake and aware in this world. Your life, no doubt, will never be the same.

ABOUT THE AUTHOR

* ✴ *

DAVID R. HAWKINS, M.D., PH.D. (1927–2012), was director of the Institute for Spiritual Research, Inc., and founder of the Path of Devotional Nonduality. He was renowned as a pioneering researcher in the field of consciousness as well as an author, lecturer, clinician, physician, and scientist. He served as an advisor to Catholic and Protestant churches, and Buddhist monasteries; appeared on major network television and radio programs; and lectured widely at such places as Westminster Abbey, the Oxford Forum, the University of Notre Dame, and Harvard University. His life was devoted to the upliftment of mankind until his death in 2012.

For more information on Dr. Hawkins's work, visit **veritaspub.com**.

Hay House Titles of Related Interest

YOU CAN HEAL YOUR LIFE, the movie,
starring Louise Hay & Friends
(available as an online streaming video)
www.hayhouse.com/louise-movie

THE SHIFT, the movie,
starring Dr. Wayne W. Dyer
(available as an online streaming video)
www.hayhouse.com/the-shift-movie

* * *

BECOMING SUPERNATURAL: How Common People Are Doing
the Uncommon, by Dr. Joe Dispenza

E-SQUARED: Nine Do-It-Yourself Energy Experiments That Prove
Your Thoughts Create Your Reality, by Pam Grout

POWER OF AWAKENING: Mindfulness Practices and Spiritual
Tools to Transform Your Life, by Dr. Wayne W. Dyer

THE SCIENCE OF SELF-EMPOWERMENT: Awakening the
New Human Story, by Gregg Braden

All of the above are available at your local bookstore,
or may be ordered by contacting Hay House (see next page).

* * *

We hope you enjoyed this Hay House book. If you'd like to receive our online catalog featuring additional information on Hay House books and products, or if you'd like to find out more about the Hay Foundation, please contact:

Hay House, Inc., P.O. Box 5100, Carlsbad, CA 92018-5100
(760) 431-7695 or (800) 654-5126
(760) 431-6948 (fax) or (800) 650-5115 (fax)
www.hayhouse.com® • www.hayfoundation.org

———

Published in Australia by: Hay House Australia Pty. Ltd.,
18/36 Ralph St., Alexandria NSW 2015
Phone: 612-9669-4299 • *Fax:* 612-9669-4144
www.hayhouse.com.au

Published in the United Kingdom by: Hay House UK, Ltd.,
The Sixth Floor, Watson House, 54 Baker Street, London W1U 7BU
Phone: +44 (0)20 3927 7290 • *Fax:* +44 (0)20 3927 7291
www.hayhouse.co.uk

Published in India by: Hay House Publishers India,
Muskaan Complex, Plot No. 3, B-2, Vasant Kunj, New Delhi 110 070
Phone: 91-11-4176-1620 • *Fax:* 91-11-4176-1630
www.hayhouse.co.in

———

Access New Knowledge.
Anytime. Anywhere.

Learn and evolve at your own pace
with the world's leading experts.

www.hayhouseU.com